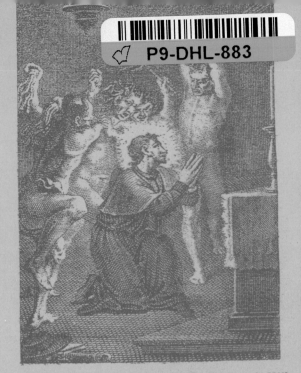

9. Au moment où il monte à l'autel pour célébrer la Sainte Messe, on lui apporte un enfant mort. Touché de pitié, il lui commande de se lever et le rend plein de vie à sa mère.

11. Priant un jour dans l'Eglise de St Thomas à Méliapor, il est assailli de violentes tentations dont il demeure vainqueur. Furieux, les démons se jettent sur lui et le frappent de verges.

SAINTS

SAINTS

A Visual Almanac of the Virtuous, Pure, Praiseworthy, and Good

Tom Morgan

CHRONICLE BOOKS
SAN FRANCISCO

ACKNOWLEDGMENTS

My sincere thanks to Annie Barrows for her knowledge of obscure medieval references and for her belief in this book. I would also like to thank Brenda Eno, Lindsay Anderson, and all the other people at Chronicle Books who helped to make this book happen.

In addition, I am grateful to Melissa Biggs, who spent hours scouring dusty bookshelves in Paris for saint illustrations, and to Reverend Richard Fowler for his inspirational guidance. Additional thanks to Jennifer Petersen, Alexandra Anderson-Spivy, and Thomas Drain for their invaluable help.

Cover: *Saint Lucy* (detail), Francesco del Cossa. Samuel H. Kress Collection, © 1993 National Gallery of Art, Washington, after 1470
Cover (small): Saint Gerard
Page 2 : Saint Anthony
Page 6 : Saint Jerome
Back Cover: Saint Sebastian

Page 174 constitutes a continuation of the copyright page.

Printed in Hong Kong.

Library of Congress Cataloging-in-Publication Data
Morgan, Tom, 1957-
    Saints: a visual almanac of the virtuous, pure, praiseworthy, and good / Tom Morgan.
          p.   cm.
    Includes index.
    ISBN 0-8118-0549-2 (hc)
    1. Christian saints—Biography. 2. Christian art and symbolism.
    I. Title.
BX4654 . M66 1994
282' . 092'2—dc20
[B]   94-7244
                                  CIP

Book and cover design: Tom Morgan, Blue Design

Distributed in Canada by Raincoast Books
8680 Cambie Street Vancouver, B.C. V6P 6M9

10 9 8 7 6 5 4 3

Chronicle Books
85 Second Street
San Francisco, CA 94105

www.chroniclebooks.com

This book is dedicated to my sweet Genevieve

CONTENTS

INTRODUCTION

This is a book that barely skims the surface of the vibrant panoply of individuals we call saints. It is estimated that over ten thousand saints have been identified by historians and hagiographers, enough to fill close to twenty volumes of the *Bibliotheca Sanctotorum*, the largest listing of saints known. Of these characters, some have been officially suppressed by the Vatican, others have fallen into historical obscurity, while others, like Patrick and Nicholas, are as widely appreciated today as they ever were.

I first became interested in the amazing histories sampled here when my wife, Genevieve, related to me the legend of the saint whose name she bears. The story of the sweet, young shepherdess from Nanterre who went on to challenge not only the savagery of Attila the Hun but also that of the Frankish leader Childeric, sparked in me a desire to learn more about these awe-inspiring yet simple people. Who were they? Having a background in art, I was familiar with the gilded images of the Renaissance, ripe with holy figures and symbols. But when it came to recognizing who they were or why they were there, I was a stranger in a strange and wonderfully mysterious land. The names of saints were familiar to me; after all, saints seem to be all around us in the names of towns, cities, streets, and mountains. I decided to write a book that would combine some of the magnificent art on this subject with the basic histories behind these personalities.

The title "saint" indicates a person who has been chosen as holy to God, and hence, someone praying to this person can be sure he or she has a direct line to the Creator's ear. Initially, saints were all martyrs, or people who died for their faith like Christ died for man's sins. Roman persecution of Christians ran rampant during the first four centuries of Christianity, and to declare one's faith meant an almost certain death; thus, many of these Christian martyrs were ultimately made into saints.

Occasionally, it was enough just to survive vicious persecution. Often miracles and cures would follow in the wake of a martyr's death, and a surge of local support would create a cult following for the deceased—a practice that was probably familiar to the descendants of the Greco-Roman polytheists. A wellspring of popular devotion was the basis for sainthood then and is the first step toward canonization now.

After Constantine declared Christian-

SAINT STEPHEN

SAINT ANTHONY

SAINT MARTHA

ity to be a tolerated religion (see Saint Helena, page 89), martrydom became rarer, and a new breed of saints cropped up: the hermits and scholars. Dedicated to achieving purity of soul in imitation of Christ, these individuals went to extraordinary lengths to deny themselves their baser instincts. Some established relatively large and lasting religious orders, some exiled themselves to the desert wilderness, while others tarried, shouting their messages over the noisy din of secular humanity. As the years progressed, more of the latter group were made saints.

Saint veneration reached its zenith during the Middle Ages. In an era of magic and superstition, relics were widely distributed, and religious pilgrimages were the most common journeys. People prayed to patron saints for help in everything from military endeavors to gout. As the Renaissance dawned, followed by the Reformation, the cult of the saints, based on miracles and faith, dimmed in the brilliance of the Age of Reason and Science.

Christianity is, in essence, a religion based on the life of a single individual: Christ. It was strengthened, however, by the belief in the sanctity of a number of individuals, the saints. At times, the widespread cult of the saints threatened to overwhelm the fledgling religion it sprang from. Not surprisingly, the church leaders strove to codify the practice of making someone a saint and developed a process that nowadays is as bureaucratic as getting a bill through Congress. Today, someone becomes a saint only through the formal process of beatification and canonization, which can occur only after the potential saint has died. The Church, more specifically the pope, hears cases for candidates to sainthood and bases its decision on how widely a candidate is supported, tangible proof of at least two miracles, and evidence of true, unselfish holiness. If approved, the saint is given a feast day and incorporated into the calendar of saints, and his or her name is formally inscribed in a canon, or list, of the saints. This inscription indicates that the Church approves the saint worthy of popular and liturgical veneration.

Despite this grueling process, saints continue to be made. These individuals and their followers stand as the touchstone of Christianity. If Jesus, the

SAINT SEBASTIAN AND SAINT FRANCIS

SAINT CHRISTOPHER

son of God—made of flesh and blood—is the physical manifestation of God on earth, then a saint, born of a man and woman, draws us mortals even closer to the divine. After all, a saint could be a neighbor, a teacher, a homeless person on the next corner. Saints were, are, and will always be, first and foremost, human. Although touched by a dedication and zeal, a holiness, not known to many of us, a saint may have a bad day, struggle with fits of anger or envy, stub a toe, or spend a pleasant day in the garden. It is this accessibility, the poignant humanity of the characters revealed in the following stories, that touches me most.

For this reason, and because I am not a theologian, a historian, or even barely religious, I have chosen to make this book a combination of fact and hearsay. Some of the saints captured here wrote detailed descriptions of their lives; some may not have existed at all. No matter, for me the important thing is that *belief* in them existed. This volume is in no shape or form an academic or exhaustive study. It is a collection of a few

of the most vivid and significant personalities, illustrated by beautiful images—some of which you may recognize, some you may not. I have purposefully filtered out doctrine and philosophy to present these figures as I see them: as simple and honest people who instigated or had visited upon them extraordinary events. The saints are arranged loosely by month in tribute to the original calendar of feast days. It is my hope that this small edition will crack a door to this wild and magical world, and that the curious will go on to read other material, visit museums, and learn more about these fabulous lives.

It is a popular custom to name one's child after the saint whose feast occurs on the day the child was born so that the child will have the benefit of that saint's protection from heaven. Edburga and Odo are not popular children's names these days, but I know I sleep a bit better with the thought of a few old Thomases on my side and a feisty little shepherdess watching over my wife. — *Tom Morgan, Saint David's Day 1994*

JANUARY

FIFTH CENTURY

SAINT ALMACHIUS

(ALSO CALLED TELEMACHUS)

Feast day: January 1

Almachius was an Eastern monk who, striving to end the gruesomely popular gladiator contests in Rome, rushed into the arena during a particularly heated battle and attempted to separate the contestants. He was promptly killed, either by the competing gladiators or by the fun-loving crowd. The emperor purportedly abolished the shows as a result of the tragedy.

FIFTH CENTURY

SAINT GENEVIEVE

Feast day: January 3. Founder and builder of Saint Denys; patroness of Paris and of little children

Attribute: A shepherd's staff and a candle, occasionally a spinning wheel

Genevieve was a young shepherdess from Nanterre who began her religious life at a very early age. In childhood she was angrily slapped by her mother, who, as a result, went blind; Genevieve miraculously restored her mother's sight with a balm of her tears. The girl grew and became known for her sanctity and virtue, taking the veil at the tender age of fifteen. Upon her parents' death, Genevieve moved to Paris, where she purportedly saved the city from being ravaged by Attila and his Huns in A.D. 451, turning them back at Orleans through fasting and prayer. She was extreme in her diet, often eating only two meals a week of beans and bread. Sometime later, when Paris was blockaded by the Franks under Childeric, the saint ran a renegade convoy up the Seine to bring back food and supplies. Winning the respect of Childeric, she charmed the release of many prisoners of war from his jails. At her death (natural), her remains were entombed in the church of Saints Peter and Paul.

In 1129 an epidemic of ergot poisoning arose in France causing mass hallucinations and convulsions. The epidemic was stayed when Genevieve's relics were carried through Paris in a public procession. Her relics were called upon often in the Middle Ages during times of great natural disaster and national crisis, and she is still invoked at such times today. Her attribute in art is usually a candle (occasionally accompanied by a satanic creature) because the devil was known to blow her candle out repeatedly when she went to pray at night, forcing her to relight it without flint or fire. Her cult is ancient, but her shrines were largely destroyed in the French Revolution.

SAINT GENEVIEVE

NINETEENTH CENTURY

SAINT ELIZABETH SETON

Feast Day: January 4

Elizabeth Bayley Seton was the first authentically American saint. Born in New York, she grew up in a wealthy, devout Episcopalian family. Her father, Richard Bayley, was a prestigious doctor, a professor at Columbia College, and the first health officer in New York. Elizabeth married a successful merchant, William Magee Seton, when she was nineteen years old. For nine years they lived together, producing five children, until William Seton died in Italy in 1803. Lonely and despairing, Elizabeth turned to Roman Catholicism. She converted in 1805 and was ostracized by her relatives as a result. To support her young children, Elizabeth started a school in New York City. At the invitation of Bishop Carroll, she moved the school to Emmitsburg, near Baltimore, Maryland, the home of Mount Saint Mary's school for boys. Elizabeth opened a free Catholic school and thus planted the seedling of American parochial education. Seton also founded Saint Joseph's College for women.

As her achievements and reputation grew, Elizabeth began to attract a large following of women supporters whom she bound together in a sisterhood entitled the American Sisters of Charity. This organization was the first American branch of the Daughters of Charity of Saint Vincent de Paul, centered in Paris. Dedicated to embodying the ideals of Saint Vincent de Paul, the Daughters of Charity were and are communities of unenclosed women who vow to give relief to the poor and teach in parish schools. Called Mother Seton by her followers, Elizabeth saw her order of nuns grow to over twenty communities by the time she died in 1821. Today, the American Sisters of Charity are still a popular and widespread organization with branches stretching throughout North and South America.

After Elizabeth's death, many miracles occured. Victims of meningitis and leukemia claimed they were cured through the saint's intervention. Elizabeth's letters and journals have been widely published.

A symbol of piety and selflessness not often typified by Americans, Seton was canonized in 1975 by Pope Paul VI, who extolled her extraordinary life as a mother, wife, and nun and celebrated her magnificent contributions to the Roman Catholic church.

FIFTH CENTURY

SAINT SIMEON

(ALSO CALLED SIMEON STYLITES)

Feast day: January 5

A truly amazing ascetic, Simeon began his life as a Syrian shepherd, joining a monastery at age thirteen. Dissatisfied with the amateur level of self-mortification, Simeon moved to a different monastery famous for its severity. There, he outfasted all the other monks by eating only once a week and almost died when a rope of twisted palm bound too tightly around his waist putrefied and had to be surgically removed. After this operation, the abbot ousted Simeon, who retired to a mountain, refusing to eat or drink anything during Lent. After his habits began to draw an unwanted throng of admirers, Simeon decided to establish himself where no one could reach him: atop a pillar that he raised progressively higher as the years passed. When he was thirty-two, the pillar he inhabited was approximately nine feet tall; by the end of his life he stood atop a pillar sixty feet high and six feet wide. Loathe to sit or lie down, except in a weakened state from prolonged fasting, Simeon wore an iron collar and rested by stooping or leaning. His colleagues were convinced that Simeon went to such extremes because of pride and decided to test him by ordering him to come down. When he prepared to obey, his fellows realized their mistake and encouraged him to stay.

SAINT SIMEON

A commanding preacher, Simeon stood at his post and prayed continuously, teaching justice and patience to an ever-growing following from the Near East. His dedication, vehemence, and extraordinary perseverance led others to emulate him and become "pillar saints," or Stylites.

SAINT HENRY OF FINLAND

Feast day: January 19. Patron of Finland

Attributes: An ax, frequently the saint standing on his murderer

Henry was a young Englishman residing in Rome who was made a bishop in Sweden in 1152 by the papal legate to Scandinavia, Cardinal Nicholas Breakspear. Following Nicholas to Sweden, Henry was present during a particularly vicious attack on the country by the Finns. He accompanied King Eric of Sweden in the counterattack, offering peace and Christianity to the pagan Finns, who refused and consequently lost the battle. A union was then created between Finland and Sweden that would last for the next two hundred years.

Henry stayed in Finland with the vanquished troops, baptizing and teaching them and building a church at Nousis. After several years, a freshly converted but still bellicose Finn named Lalli killed a Swedish soldier and was excommunicated by Henry. Lalli was so enraged that he turned on Henry, killing him with an ax. Henry's life and miracles are vividly depicted in statue, stained glass, and paintings throughout medieval Finnish churches. Predominantly called upon by the native seal fishermen during violent storms at sea, he is frequently shown trampling on the ax-wielding Lalli.

THIRD CENTURY

SAINT SEBASTIAN

Feast day: January 20: One of the Fourteen Holy

Helpers; patron of archers and soldiers

Attribute: Arrows

Sebastian was a nobleman, born in Narbonne, who served around A.D. 283 in the Praetorian Guard and was a favorite of emperor Diocletian. He practiced Christianity in secret, and was a success in the military (he was promoted to captain) until he witnessed the horrendous torture of his friends and fellow Christians, Mark and Marcellian. Moved to speak out, he converted many with his conviction. To punish Sebastian, Diocletian decreed that he should be shot to death with arrows. Sebastian miraculously revived after the execution and reproached the emperor for his cruelty. The emperor promptly ordered Sebastian

to be beaten to death with clubs and his body thrown into the sewers of Rome. His body was recovered and buried near the relics of Saint Peter and Saint Paul. The church of Saint Sebastiano now stands on the Via Appia in Rome.

Sebastian was a favorite hero of Renaissance painters, who often portrayed him as a young, effeminate, male nude. Representations of Saint Sebastian go back as far as the seventh century. In these early works, and some later ones, he is depicted as an elderly man with a beard, wearing a crown of thorns. He is also envisioned as a knight holding an arrow. The more familiar images of Sebastian—tied to a tree, stake, or cross—being pierced with arrows, came about during the fifteenth century.

The patron saint of archers and soldiers, Sebastian was also invoked against the plague, which was said to strike as quickly and be as deadly as an arrow.

SAINT PAUL

Feast day: January 25, joint feast with Peter on
June 29. One of the apostles
Attributes: The sword, often depicted pointing down;
a book; and letters (representing his epistles).

Born to the name Saul, Saint Paul was originally Jewish but became the preacher of Christianity to the Gentiles after his conversion. Paul spent the first part of his life viciously persecuting Christians (Christianity was illegal until the fourth century), chasing them down, imprisoning them, and killing them: indeed, he was a facilitator of and witness to the stoning of Saint Stephen. Saul was on his way to Damascus to root out more Christians when his famous conversion occurred. Traveling down the middle of the road, he suddenly saw a vision of Jesus that blinded him. He was cured of his blindness after three

days in Damascus and was baptized, taking the name Paul. He then proceeded to preach Christianity as vociferously as he had persecuted it. His former colleagues in stoning, now turned enemies, were so hostile to him that they lay in wait at the gates of Damascus to capture the "traitor." He escaped by being lowered over the walls of the city in a basket, an act of cowardice of which he later boasted.

Paul cured the blind and the paralytic, and fourteen of the epistles in the Bible are attributed to him. He is described as a physically unimpressive individual who had a bald head and bowed legs, but whose visible loftiness of spirit and mind transcended his body.

Many miracles are attributed to Paul, and these are widely depicted in art: He was thrown to the beasts in Rome but was protected by a lion, whom he later baptized; during one period of incarceration, an earthquake supposedly shook open the doors of his cell; when he and some companions were being taken to Rome to stand trial, their ship was wrecked off the Island of Malta, and the Christians swam to safety; and when a poisonous snake reportedly wrapped itself around his hand, Paul shook the asp off into a fire. Paul was eventually executed, perhaps with Saint Peter, and upon his beheading, milk flowed from his neck over the executioner's clothing. His severed head bounced on the ground three times, and at each spot a fountain instantaneously gushed forth. The site is now called Tre Fontana.

Saint Paul and Saint Peter are the founders of the Church of Rome. Pictured together, they generally stand for this patronage.

FIFTH CENTURY

SAINT PAULA

Feast day: January 26. Patroness of widows

Widowed and wealthy at the age of thirty-two, Paula endured a period of great sorrow exacerbated by the death of her daughter Blesilla. She experienced an extreme religious conversion to Christianity and adopted a regimen of prayer, austere diet, and rest. She renounced all social amusements and gave her money to the poor. When she met Saint Jerome, Paula left Rome to travel to Bethlehem. Together they built a monastery and convent with a guest house for pilgrims and maintained a popular salon for religious intellectuals. Paula also participated in Saint Jerome's translation of the Bible, the *Vulgate.*

FOURTH CENTURY

SAINT ANTHONY

Feast day: January 27. Father of monks

Attributes: A monk's cowl, the devil in the form of a

wild beast, a pig, and a bell

Anthony of the Desert was a wealthy Egyptian man who, after seeing to it that his sister was properly educated, gave away everything he possessed and moved into the desert. Living a life of severe deprivation, Anthony wore a haircloth, slept little, and ate only once a day, a meal of bread and water. The devil put lusty thoughts in the saint's head by appearing to him in the shape of a frolicking, beautiful, half-dressed maiden. Anthony was also attacked by the devil in the form of hyenas and other savage beasts. The saint, despite these torments of the flesh, remained steadfast in his ideals, performing strict penances.

His seclusion and severe habits encouraged many admirers who often spent days in the desert searching for Anthony, and upon finding him, refused to leave. To shelter this throng, Anthony established two monasteries that were the first ever to be founded. To this day he has been considered the father of all monks.

Anthony was divinely inspired to seek out the elderly and dying Saint Paul (the hermit's hermit) in the desert. It was customary for a raven to bring a half of a loaf of bread daily to Saint Paul, but at the moment of Anthony and Paul's auspicious meeting, the same raven dropped an entire loaf of bread from the sky and Paul passed away. A lion appeared and dug a grave for the saint; Paul was buried in a shroud Anthony lovingly draped over him. When Anthony was ninety, he died in the desert and was buried, as he requested, in a unmarked grave.

Anthony is usually accompanied in iconography by a pig, a symbol of his

lewd thoughts, and a bell, which he used to frighten the devil. In addition, these emblems were adopted by the Order of the Hospitallers of Saint Anthony in the twelfth century. A mecca for sufferers of ergot poisoning (also called Saint Anthony's Fire), the members of the Order were permitted to let their pigs run free, and they walked the streets ringing little bells to attract alms. The tau cross adorned their black robes, and Anthony may be seen in art wearing the same.

Saint Anthony of Padua, a Franciscan friar who lived at the turn of the thirteenth century, was a renowned miracle worker and preacher, and was very generous with the poor. Saint Anthony's Bread, a Victorian institution that clothes and feeds the starving, is still present today. Saint Anthony's Fair is held on June 13, his feast day. He is generally portrayed in art with a lily and a book, or preaching to the fishes. His remains lie in Padua, Italy. Saint Anthony is invoked to help the absent-minded find lost objects.

FEBRUARY

FIFTH CENTURY

SAINT BRIGID

(ALSO CALLED BRIDE)

Feast day: February 1. Founder of Kildare; patroness of poets, blacksmiths, and midwives

Attribute: A cow

Brigid of Ireland was a robust and immensely energetic young woman who performed many miracles and contributed significantly to the spread of Christianity in Ireland. Best described by some as a sort of nun-cowgirl, Brigid was the daughter of a pagan father. Brigid's mother was a Christian servant in her father's household. Brigid, perhaps in response to her mother's oppressed state, spent most of her adult life gathering together women from all over Ireland into protected monastic communities.

On all accounts, Brigid was a saint to be reckoned with. A miracle worker of great power, she was legendary for her abilities to multiply food : turning bath water into beer and milking her cows successfully three times a day. She cheerfully performed the hard labor of her agricultural life,

wearing many hats with ease: cowherd, butter-churner, baker, and corn reaper, among others. Brigid lived into her seventies and was buried in Downpatrick. A fire around her shrine at Kildare was kept burning for centuries, fueled by devoted members of her community of nuns. The fire was encircled by a ring of bushes through which no man was allowed to pass.

Second in popularity in Ireland only to Saint Patrick, Brigid inspired a cult that spread throughout Flanders, Portugal, France, Italy, and Wales.

Many churches are dedicated to her, and especially in Wales, Saint Bride's Day is still celebrated with great enthusiasm.

Brigid is often shown in art with a cow at her feet, symbolizing her affinity for nature and her days spent in the cow pastures. She has also been linked with the pagan goddess Brig, whose name means courage and strength and whose cult was celebrated with a ceremony of fire. Brigid has experienced a relatively recent resurgence in popularity due to the interest of contemporary feminist and environmental groups, as well as the growing women's movement in Ireland.

FOURTH CENTURY
SAINT BLAISE

Feast day: February 3. One of the Fourteen Holy
Helpers; patron of sore-throat sufferers and wool-carders
Attributes: The wool comb and two crossed candles

The son of noble Christians, Blaise became a bishop in Armenia at an early age but was forced to hide in a cave to avoid persecution under the pagan emperor Licinius. Wild animals gathered around his cave to partake of food and conversation with him; he was famous for blessing and curing sick and wounded animals. Blaise was also responsible for healing a boy with a fishbone stuck in his throat. Later, when Blaise was imprisoned, the boy's mother visited him, bringing food and the candles with which he is often depicted. Blaise was martyred by having his flesh torn apart by iron combs before he was beheaded (hence his appeal to wool-carders).

Popular since the eighth century, Blaise's cult still flourishes in some parts of the world. In the blessing of Saint Blaise, which still takes place, those who suffer from diseases of the throat are treated by placing two crossed, lighted candles at their throats. It is also customary to treat sick cattle with water sanctified by the blessing of Saint Blaise.

THIRD CENTURY
SAINT AGATHA

Feast day: February 5. Patroness of Catania, Sicily,
and bell-founders
Attributes: Pincers, a knife, a torch or candle, and
carrying her two breasts on a plate

Agatha was a well-born Sicilian girl who consecrated her virginity to Christ and spurned the affections of the worldly Quintian, a Roman consul. Spitefully, Quintian decreed imperial edicts against Christianity and handed the maid over to a notorious local brothel-keeper to teach her a lesson. Agatha, determined to retain her purity, resisted the brothel-keeper's corruption. She was tortured on the rack and had both her breasts either torn or cut off. In her agony, she saw Saint Peter in a vision and he helped to heal her wounds. She died in jail after being roasted over live coals. Agatha is often invoked against earthquakes and fires (thus her attributes related to fire), and her veil was used to help keep the flow of lava from destroying her hometown of Catania, Sicily, after the eruption of Mount Etna. She is also a protectress against breast disease and a patroness of bell-founders. The latter patronage arose from the many images depicting the saint holding a tray carrying her inverted breasts, which often look like bells or dome-shaped loaves of bread. In some cultures, it was customary to celebrate Saint Agatha's day by bringing small round loaves of bread to church to be blessed.

FOURTH CENTURY

SAINT DOROTHY

Feast day: February 6

Attribute: A basket of fruit and flowers

A much-beloved saint, particularly in Germany and Italy, Dorothy was persecuted under emperor Diocletian for refusing to marry or to worship idols. On her way to her execution, a lawyer named Theophilus heckled her from the sidelines, mockingly asking her to send him some of the fruits and the flowers from the garden of paradise. She agreed, and at the moment of Dorothy's earthly departure, an angel appeared and gave Theophilus a basket containing three apples and three roses. The lawyer was instantly converted and later died as a martyr.

Her story has inspired poems by Swinburne and Gerard Manley Hopkins, a poet who was ordained in 1877.

SIXTEENTH CENTURY

SAINT PAUL MIKI

AND COMPANIONS

Feast day: February 6. First martyrs of the Far East

Twenty-six people, including Saint Paul Miki, were crucified in Japan after having parts of their left ears cut off and displayed in various towns to terrify the more than two thousand other Christians living there in 1597. Paul Miki was a Japanese aristocrat, a Jesuit, and a renowned preacher. He was put to death with two fellow Jesuits, six Franciscans, and seventeen laymen, laywomen, and children. All twenty-six were bound to crosses alive, planted in the ground in a row, and then hastily done in by twenty-six separate executioners. As dictated by a particularly gruesome Japanese custom of the times, every member of their families was doomed to death as well. Originally celebrated only in Japan, Saint Paul Miki's feast day became part of the calendar of the Church in 1970.

THIRD CENTURY

SAINT APOLLONIA

Feast day: February 9. Patroness of dentists

Attribute: A tooth in pair of pincers

There are many different accounts of the life of Apollonia. In one version, she was an elderly virgin who was dragged out of her home by a rioting mob and struck across the jaw, which knocked out all her teeth. Threatening to burn her alive, Apollonia's enemies demanded that she renounce her faith. The old woman heroically broke free and, without hesitation, threw herself into the nearby blaze.

In a different tale, Apollonia was a king's daughter whose father tortured her by pulling out all her teeth, one by one. She promised, upon her deathbed, to help all those with toothaches.

Artists often render her as a young, beautiful maiden holding a tooth in a pair of pincers; she is also pictured bound to a stake while one torturer

SAINT APOLLONIA

SAINT VALENTINE

holds her hair and another forcibly removes her teeth. A modern manifestation of her legend is the publication of a dentist's quarterly entitled *The Apollonian.*

THIRD CENTURY
SAINT VALENTINE

Feast day: February 14. Patron of lovers

There are actually two Valentines recorded in history, and neither has much to do with lovers or courting. One was a Roman priest martyred under Claudius, and the other a bishop of Ternis martyred in Rome. February 14 is historically the time of year when birds mate, which may have inspired the romantic association, but the practice of picking a valentine is widely believed to be left over from a mid-February Roman festival in honor of the goddess Juno, when boys drew by lot the names of unmarried girls and then playfully beat them with swatches of soft goat hide to guarantee their purity.

THIRTEENTH CENTURY
SAINT MARGARET OF CORTONA

Feast day: February 22

Attribute: A bush and a little dog

Margaret was so severely mistreated by her stepmother that she left home and became the mistress of a knight in Montepulciano, living openly with him for nine years and bearing him a son. One day her little dog pulled at her skirts and led her to the body of her lover under a bush, murdered by his rivals for Margaret's favors.

Rejected by her unsympathetic stepmother and overcome with grief for her

SAINT MARGARET

lover, Margaret blamed her beauty and vanity for the death and decided to repent. Walking barefoot, with a rope about her neck, she carried her son to the doors of a Franciscan convent in Cortona.

Margaret's beauty and charm were such that, combined with her reputation, the friars had to be convinced of her good intentions. To prove herself, she tirelessly nursed the sick and poor and practiced extreme personal penitence: fasting, wearing hair shirts, depriving herself of sleep, and mutilating her body. She eventually earned her way into the convent and knew herself to be truly forgiven her past debauchery when the figure of Christ on the crucifix supposedly leaned toward her while she knelt before him in prayer.

MARCH

THIRD CENTURY

SAINTS PERPETUA AND FELICITY

Feast day: March 6. Saints of the Roman Canon

Perpetua, a wealthy married woman with a son, and Felicity, the pregnant wife of her slave, were arrested with fellow Christians Secondulus and Saturninus soon after a law was passed in Carthage that forbade any new conversions to Christianity. Felicity gave birth to a daughter in prison. Perpetua experienced many inspirational visions while imprisoned and withstood her ordeal so heroically that she converted her jailer. Sentenced to die by being thrown to wild beasts at the "games," the prisoners were led joyfully to their doom in the official arena. Perpetua, who refused to wear the blasphemous tunic of Ceres, was in such an advanced state of ecstasy that she was unaware of injury when a mad heifer gored her. Saturninus was mangled by a leopard, and Felicity was trampled, but not hurt, by a bull. Soon the crowd grew weary of the beasts' failure to kill the Christians and demanded that they be dispatched with no further ado by a sword to the throat. With one final kiss, Felicity and Perpetua made their farewells to each other. Such was Perpetua's strength of mind that she guided the gladiator's sword to her own neck.

FIFTEENTH CENTURY

SAINT COLETTE

(ALSO CALLED NICOLETTE)

Feast day: March 6

The daughter of a carpenter in Picardy, Colette was a sickly child who went on to become a Franciscan nun and had great success reforming the convents of the Poor Clares. Like Saint Francis, she had a passion for nature. She also built convents in Flanders and France.

THIRD CENTURY

SAINT MAXIMILIAN

Feast day: March 12

One of the earliest conscientious objectors, twenty-one-year-old Maximilian, the son of a war veteran, was drafted, in customary tradition, into the Roman army. Maximilian announced to the proconsul (and to his disappointed father) that he would not serve his country, as his only loyalty was to the army of God. When it was pointed out that he must serve or perish, he chose death, replying that it would mean eternal life with God. His name was struck from the army roster and he was condemned. At his beheading, Maximilian noted the shabby dress of his executioner and, calling to his father, requested that his own, new clothes be stripped from his body and given to the impoverished man.

FIRST CENTURY

SAINT LONGINUS

Feast day: March 15. Patron of Mantua, Italy

Attribute: A spear

Standing guard at the Crucifixion, Longinus, described as having a malady of the eyes, used his lance to pierce the side of Christ and then rubbed his eyes with his hands, which were covered in the blood that had run down his spear. Instantly his sight was restored to him, and he became a Christian. Longinus was baptized by the apostles and martyred when he refused to sacrifice to pagan gods. On the day of his execution, he was brought before a governor who was blind. Longinus promised that after his death the governor's sight would be returned. Longinus was beheaded, and the governor converted and regained his sight. Saint Longinus appears in art carrying a spear, standing or mounted on a horse. He is the patron of Mantua because, to encourage the conversion of the Mantuans, he supposedly sent the city a vial containing drops of Christ's blood. His alleged relics are at Mantua.

FOURTH CENTURY

SAINT PATRICK

Feast day: March 17. Archbishop of Armagh; patron of Ireland

Attributes: Frequently depicted dressed in a bishop's cloak, holding a staff and a shamrock, and treading on snakes.

British by birth, Patrick was the son of a town counselor who was a deacon. When he was sixteen or seventeen, Patrick was kidnapped by marauders

and taken to Ireland, where he was sold into slavery and spent the next six years of his life suffering under extreme duress. One night he was told in a dream that he would escape his owner, triumph over many hardships, and finally return to freedom in his homeland. Fueled by this thought, Patrick ran away from his master and traveled two hundred miles to a port, where he begged for passage on a ship to Gaul. The sailors initially denied his request, but mysteriously relented at the last minute. After three days at sea and a month traversing wilderness on foot, Patrick reached his home and was reunited with his family.

Patrick entered the priesthood in France, joining a monastary at Lérins, and later became a bishop after years of study at Auxerre. During this time, Patrick began to have visions telling him to go back to Ireland and spread his faith. Conveniently, the missionary bishop in Ireland, Saint Palladius, had recently died, and in 432 Patrick was consecrated in his place. Working primarily in the north, Patrick strove to abolish the idolatry, paganism, and sun worship of the Irish Druids. In one celebrated event, Patrick defied the pagan priests of Tara by spontaneously kindling an Easter fire on the hillside of Slane. At first offended by this audacious act, the high king, King Laoghaire, grew to respect the temerarious saint who explained Christianity to him by demonstrating the mystery of the Trinity with a shamrock.

Although he encouraged the Irish to become nuns and monks, Patrick never became one himself. Sensitive to his own lack of education, Patrick built the Cathedral Church in Armagh, which became a center for education and administration. Patrick was remarkably successful in his mission, converting almost the entire island region by region before he died in 461, and helping to recodify the ancient laws defining slavery and taxation of the poor. Patrick was buried in Downpatrick, which was an important holy shrine until it was destroyed by the British in 1539.

The powers of Saint Patrick are phenomenal. He

is able to release seven souls from purgatory every Thursday and twelve each Saturday. On Judgment Day, he will lead the souls of Ireland to the Judgment Seat. On a more earthly plain, the National Museum of Dublin has a shrine entombing the remains of his bell and a solitary tooth. Saint Patrick's Day is still uproariously celebrated throughout America. A symbol of patriotism for the Irish, Saint Patrick's Day is an Irish national holiday and a holy day when all the pubs are closed and worshippers are obliged to

attend Mass. Saint Patrick is renowned in legend for driving the serpents out of Ireland with a staff given to him by Jesus.

SEVENTH CENTURY

SAINT CUTHBERT

Feast day: March 20

Cuthbert was a shepherd near Edinburgh, Scotland, who became a hermit and was unable to find a place remote enough for his liking. Initially settling on Saint Cuthbert's Isle, he retreated farther to the wilds of the Inner Farne and built a narrow cell in Lindisfarne. A great lover of nature and natural history, Cuthbert was a protector of sea birds and had an ability to communicate with all animals.

He tamed the wild ducks of the Inner

Farne. In Scotland and northern England, a certain species of seaweed is called "St. Cuthbert's Beads," and eiderdown is commonly referred to as "cuddy's ducks." The Farne Islands are a national refuge for birds, seals, and other wildlife, due in part, perhaps, to Cuthbert's protection.

THIRTEENTH CENTURY

Saint Thomas Aquinas

Feast day: March 28. Doctor of the Church; patron of booksellers

Attribute: The sun

Thomas Aquinas was born to a noble family and educated at the University of Naples. Known as "the dumb ox" to his fellow students, Thomas was drawn to the intellectual bent of the Dominicans and decided to become an impoverished friar—a career plan that shocked and disappointed his family, who were hoping he would contribute to his inheritance by landing a cushy ecclesiastical position somewhere. His family locked Thomas away to convince him to change his mind. His brothers attempted to distract him by sending a prostitute into his chamber to seduce him. Thomas responded by pulling a brand from the fire and drawing the sign of the cross on the chimney. With the burning stick in his hand, he chased the woman from his room. For his triumph, an angel appeared and tied a cord around his waist, and he was freed from temptations of the flesh.

After two years, his family came to see the error of their ways and freed Thomas to follow his true calling. Thomas Aquinas is credited with the foundation of all modern Christian thought. Expressing theology through philosophical principles that were decidely Aristotelian, Thomas Aquinas explained that reason and faith are two separate but harmonious realms where the truths of faith co-exist with

SAINT THOMAS AQUINAS

and complement those of reason. With this philosophy, Aquinas triumphed over two opposing schools of thought: the Averroists (who would separate truth and faith absolutely) and the Augustinians (who would make truth a matter of faith). Thus, Thomas Aquinas opened the portals of acceptability to Aristotelian thought, which had up to that point been considered heretical.

A consummate intellectual, Thomas was constantly at work: thinking, writing, and preaching about philosophy and theology. Often in the middle of conversations, his eyes would glaze over as he became lost in some train of thought. His *Summa Theologica* is the cornerstone of Catholic doctrine. Thomas Aquinas died at the early age of forty-nine by tripping over a tree.

In art, Thomas Aquinas is frequently drawn holding a book from which rays of divine light issue forth. His remains lie in Toulouse, France.

Another Saint Thomas (feast day: December 21), the apostle, was the original "Doubting Thomas" because he refused to believe in the Resurrection until Christ appeared to him, inviting Thomas to touch his wounds. He is connected to missionary work in India, and is often depicted in art holding a T square, symbolic of the spiritual palace he built for an Indian king after donating all the funds for the construction of the physical palace to the poor. He occasionally holds a spear, the weapon of his martyrdom, and is invoked against blindness. He is the patron saint of architects.

One more of the many other saint Thomases was Thomas à Becket, Archbishop of Canterbury under the impetuous King Henry II of England. A man of great political power, Thomas was elected chancellor when the twenty-one-year-old king succeeded to the throne. Thomas became a confidant and intimate friend of the king, and was considered to be the second most powerful man in the kingdom. In gratitude, Thomas often went up against his own church in

support of the king, voicing no opposition to an increased taxation on his own fellow churchmen.
When Henry II appointed Thomas archbishop, their
relationship changed drastically. Thomas initially
refused the appointment, but later accepted after the
king's insistence.

Upon his appointment to archbishop, the once
carefree chancellor adopted an ascetic way of life.
Thomas declined the king's payments of luxury and
entertainment in the hope of embodying the ideals
inherent in his new duty. Strengthened by his faith,
Thomas began to challenge his king on all matters
financial, spiritual, and political. Endless conflicts
and arguments ensued that boiled down to a struggle
for power (and money) between church and state.
Fearing for his safety, Thomas fled to France in 1164
to appeal to the pope. Six years later, in December of
1170, the king and the archbishop reached a make-
shift truce and Thomas returned to England.
However, trouble immediately surfaced. Henry had

actually been crowned by the archbishop of York in
direct violation of constitutional law and precedent.
Thomas objected strenuously and, upon landing in
England, demanded the resignations of the bishops
who had participated in the coronation.

In a matter of days, Henry's response to this latest
imbraglio was to demand from his courtiers, "Will no
one rid me of this troublesome priest?" On December
29, four swordsmen took the king at his word and as-
sassinated the archbishop while he knelt in his own
cathedral. Thomas's tomb immediately became a
shrine and hundreds of miracles followed his death.
All of Europe was outraged by the nefarious crime.
Henry II was forced to perform public penance for
the murder, but lost little of his political power. Hundreds of years later, Henry VIII suppressed Thomas's
feast, defaced his image, and removed his name from
all liturgical calendars. Nevertheless, Thomas of
Canterbury has remained an enduring and important
English saint. Saint Thomas was canonized in 1173.

SAINT MARY OF EGYPT

The pilgrimage from London to Canterbury was an immensely popular journey in the Middle Ages until Thomas's shrine was destroyed by Henry VIII in 1538; the Pilgrim's Way is immortalized in Chaucer's *Canterbury Tales.* T. S. Eliot's *Murder in the Cathedral* is a poetic dramatization of the saint's murder.

FIFTH CENTURY

SAINT MARY OF EGYPT

Feast day: April 2

One of the lesser-known saint Marys, Mary of Egypt was a prostitute, working for seventeen years on the streets of Alexandria. Mary decided to go on a pilgrimage to Jerusalem. Penniless, she bought her passage by allowing the sailors to have their way with her during the ship's voyage. In Jerusalem, when confronted with an icon of the Virgin Mary, she became ashamed of her profession. Mary wandered out into the desert and remained there for fifty years. She was found by a sympathetic monk, Zossima, who blessed her. With this she was forgiven and died.

THIRD CENTURY

SAINT ACACIUS

Feast day: March 31. One of the Fourteen Holy Helpers

Attribute: A crown of thorns

Put to death along with ten thousand companions on the summit of Mount Ararat, Acacius may have been a bishop. At his death, he claimed that anyone who prayed to him might have good health in body and soul. For this reason, and because he is always depicted with a crown of thorns, Saint Acacius is invoked against headaches.

FIFTEENTH CENTURY

SAINT VINCENT FERRER

Feast day: April 5. Patron saint of builders

Attribute: A trumpet

A transplanted Englishman who grew up in Valencia, Spain, Vincent Ferrer was noted for his booming loud voice, his gift for speaking in tongues, and his skill at saving sinners and converting new Christians with his terrifying sermons on the Last Judgment and the horrors of hell. He journeyed far and wide throughout Europe, often preaching in open spaces to the vast crowds he drew.

During his travels the saint was supposedly invited to dine in a small French town with a local woman, who, in a fury, had chopped up her son and served the boy for dinner. When the mother confessed her deed, the saint quickly reassembled the boy and restored him to life. He also resurrected another boy who fell off a wall while listening to a particularly mesmerizing sermon. Called the "Angel of Judgment" for his electrifying sermons, Vincent Ferrer is often depicted in art with wings; the trumpet he uses to call sinners is often pictured as well.

FOURTH CENTURY

SAINT GEORGE

Feast day: April 23. One of the Fourteen Holy Helpers; patron saint of England, soldiers, knights (specifically the Order of the Garter), boy scouts, archers, armorers, and husbands (as protectors of women)

Attribute: A dragon

The original model for chivalric behavior, Saint George was immensely popular and his legend widespread throughout Europe for centuries. The tale is

SAINT GEORGE

this: A poisonous dragon was terrorizing the country-side, killing anyone close enough for it to breathe on. Its fury was assuaged only by a daily sacrifice of sheep. When all the sheep were eaten, the citizens ruefully turned to human sacrifice. A lottery was established, and when the lots were drawn, the king's daughter picked the losing ticket. The girl went toward her fate in a bridal gown and was tied to the mouth of the dragon's cave at the edge of the sea. As the dragon appeared, George swooped down astride his white stallion and attacked, piercing the beast with his lance until it surrendered. Then he led it to town by the princess's girdle, captive and docile. George offered to slay the dragon in exchange for a mass conversion to Christianity. The king complied and baptized his entire citizenry. George refused any reward, asking that the money be distributed to the poor instead.

George's cult grew during the Crusades, fueled by numerous visions of the saint during the heat of battle. Richard I invoked Saint George for protection, and it

is his cross (red on a white ground) that appears on England's flag. Henry V declared him the official patron of England during the Battle of Agincourt. At various times in the Middle Ages, Venice, Portugal, and Genoa all did the same. He is a symbol of British nobility, nationalism, and leadership in times of war and is often called upon to protect against the plague, leprosy, and syphilis.

THIRTEENTH CENTURY

SAINT ZITA

(ALSO CALLED SITHA, CITHA)

Feast day: April 27. Patroness of Lucca, Italy,
and domestic servants
Attribute: A ring of keys

Zita worked from the age of twelve, and for forty years thereafter, as a maid in the house of a wool merchant in Italy. She toiled fervently, gave food away to the poor, and dedicated herself to good works—none of which endeared her to her fellow servants or her masters during most of her servitude. Often harangued and punished for her deeds, she eventually won the kindness and respect of her employers, who witnessed some of the miracles occurring in the course of her duties: A pitcher of water turned to wine when she gave it to a pilgrim; a loaf of bread that she had taken from the larder to give to a starving family burst into bloom when her master confronted her with the theft; and when she borrowed her master's cloak to give to a freezing beggar, it was returned to her by an angel. She is invoked to help find lost keys.

MAY

FIRST CENTURY

SAINT JAMES THE LESSER

Feast day: May 3. Apostle

Attribute: A club

There are actually two Saint Jameses who were apostles during the first century: James the Greater and James the Lesser. James the Lesser might have been the brother of Jesus, and the Epistle of Saint James is attributed to him. This James may also have been the first bishop in Jerusalem, who was so devastated by Jesus' death that he vowed not to eat until the Second Coming. Jesus supposedly appeared to James, cooked him a meal, and relieved him of his vow James the Lesser was a strict ascetic—often praying for such lengths of time that his knees turned as knotty and hard as a camel's. James the Lesser was sentenced to death by stoning, but when he was arrested inside the temple of Jerusalem, he was thrown off the temple roof and, upon landing, beaten to death by a club.

Saint James the Greater (feast day: July 25) was the brother of Saint John the Apostle. The two brothers were among the first of Jesus' followers and were witness to most of Jesus' miracles. James the Greater was killed by a sword and is thus pictured with one in art. In his legend, James was being led to his death when the soldier accompanying him, overwhelmed with his prisoner's dignity and grace, fell to his knees and confessed his Christianity. The saint reportedly raised him, kissed him, and said, "Peace be with you," and both men were executed together. For this reason, James is attributed with the inclusion in the Eucharist of "The Peace," a ritual in which members of a congregation turn and greet one another with, "Peace be with you."

FOURTH CENTURY
SAINT FLORIAN

Feast day: May 4. Patron of Poland, Linz, and Upper Austria

Florian was an Austrian soldier in the Roman army who was able to stop a huge blazing fire with only a bucketful of water. He turned himself in as a Christian to the local governor and was consequently thrown into the river Enns with a stone around his neck. He is called upon to protect against floods and fire.

FIRST CENTURY

NEREUS AND ACHILLEUS

Feast day: May 12

As Roman soldiers, Nereus and Achilleus were intimidated into carrying out the despotic orders of a cruel, tyrannical commander. At some point, they were converted to Christianity and left the military life altogether to become eunuchs and serve the lady Flavia Domitilla (a relative of the emperor Domitian), who lived in exile. Eventually, they were martyred for refusing to sacrifice to idols.

ACHILLEUS

FOURTEENTH CENTURY

SAINT YVES

(ALSO CALLED IVES, IVO, IVA; FEMININE
FORM IS YVONNE, EVE, AND EVA)

Feast day: May 19. Patron of lawyers

*Attribute: Lawyer's robe with Franciscan cord and
an angel or dove*

Yves was a lawyer from Brittany who represented
widows and orphans for free. Artists generally render him standing between two impoverished
litigants, his back turned against the bribe of a rich
man's proffered purse filled with gold. An angel or
dove occasionally floats nearby.

There is also another Saint Yves (feast day: April
24), whose tomb lies near a spring in England that has
curative powers. Another saint, Ia or Ives (feast day:
February 3), sailed from Ireland to Cornwall on a leaf.

FIFTEENTH CENTURY

SAINT RITA

*Feast day: May 22. Patroness of desperate causes,
especially those involving marital trouble*

A long-suffering woman who had always in-
tended to be a nun but was forced to marry an
extremely ill-tempered man instead, Rita withstood
eighteen years of his violent temper, beatings, infi-
delities, and insults, in the process bearing him two
sons. After her tormentor was brought home dead
one night, the victim of some nefarious vendetta, her
two sons, bent on revenge, went after their father's
murderer. Rita prayed that her sons might die rather
than prolong the cycle of violence. Her prayers were
answered. Rita thankfully joined a convent.

Soon after taking the veil, Rita's constant prayer
and self-mortification, combined with intensive
meditation on the Passion of Christ, caused a small

gash to open on her forehead that would not heal for the remaining fifteen years of her life. Rita counseled sinners and took care of sick nuns, dying herself of tuberculosis. Her patronage of desperate causes (similar to Saint Jude) has made her very popular; she is called upon particularly often by women suffering severe marital problems. Her following extends today throughout Europe, South America, and the Philippines.

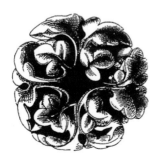

THIRTEENTH CENTURY

SAINT WILLIAM

Feast day: May 23

William of Rochester was a fisherman who became a Christian in his youth. He was committed to caring for orphans and poor children, and once saved a baby deserted at a church door. His love for children was his undoing when he took a boy from an orphanage with him on his journey to Jerusalem. When they passed through Rochester the boy suggested a deserted short cut. Once they were off the main road, the boy seized the opportunity and killed William, robbing the saint of what little he had. A crazy woman found the body and was cured of her madness by decorating it with garlands of honeysuckle.

Other Williams are William Firmatus, who is invoked by farmers to protect their crops from raiding creatures, and William of York, an archbishop who was allegedly poisoned in his cathedral at York.

FIFTEENTH CENTURY

SAINT JOAN OF ARC

Feast day: May 30

Attributes: Armor, holding a banner and a sword

Brought up at the height of the Hundred Years War, Joan was the pious daughter of a farmer in Champagne, France. One day, while she was out tending the fields, Joan heard voices from heaven telling her that she was destined to save France from the English. Joan believed the voices to be those of Catherine of Alexandria, Margaret of Antioch, and the archangel Michael. The voices gave Joan no rest until she was able to convince the local government to take her to see the dauphin (the prince who became Charles VII). The dauphin was in disguise, but Joan easily recognized him—thanks to her saintly advisors—and impressed upon him the nature of her visitations. Charles became convinced of her author-

ity and listened when she directed him to send more troops to Orléans. Joan led the renewed battalions to victory, saving Orléans and capturing some English forts. She was wounded superficially in the battle, by a lance to her breast, but she persevered, urging the men onward with her courage and conviction.

When Charles was crowned king, Joan stood by his side approvingly, heedless to warnings that she was annoying the masculine forces ruling the court and church halls. The warnings came home to roost during a battle when the Duke of Burgundy captured the saint. Fickle Charles abandoned her, and the Duke sold Joan to the English. Unable to condemn Joan for beating them in battle, the English turned her over to a British inquisitional court at Rouen, where she was tried for witchcraft and heresy (the forces to which the losers credited her extraordinary accomplishments). She was denied entrance to a church, Mass, or the Sacrament, and she was ceaselessly questioned for days by ruthless inquisitors. Despite her peasant's lack of education and vocabulary, Joan was able to defend herself admirably against a team of theologians, but eventually she was worn down and forced to recant her "demonic" visions and wear a skirt instead of armor. True to her nature, Joan only briefly obeyed these mandates and soon resumed dressing as a man. She was promptly proclaimed a lapsed heretic and burnt at the stake in what would later be called a gross political crime endorsed by the Church.

George Bernard Shaw wrote the play *Saint Joan* about her. Saint Joan has been venerated by feminists and women's rights activists for generations. Regardless of people's interpretations, Joan is a symbol of great patriotism, strength, and faith. Artists inevitably render her in full armor in the heat of battle or being burnt at the stake. The *Fête de Jeanne D'Arc* takes place in France on the second Sunday in May.

JUNE

FOURTH CENTURY

SAINT ERASMUS

(ALSO CALLED ELMO AND TELMO)

Feast day: June 2. One of the Fourteen Holy Helpers; patron of sailors and children with colic

Attribute: A windlass

According to legend, Erasmus was a bishop in Syria who fled persecution by emperor Diocletian, becoming a hermit on Mount Lebanon. He was discovered there, taken away, beaten, rolled in pitch, and set on fire. Surviving this agony, he was summoned by the archangel Michael and ordered to preach in Italy. There he was imprisoned near Gaeta, between Rome and Naples, and martyred by having his intestines wrapped around a windlass. Thus, he has become a patron to those with bowel trouble.

Sailors invoke Saint Elmo for safe passage through stormy waters. Often, just before or right after a thunder-and-lightning storm at sea, a bluish electrical tinge can be seen around the masthead; sailors anxiously look for "Saint Elmo's fire" to signify that their ship has been taken under his protection. The source of Erasmus's legend, however, comes from a sermon the bishop completed during a fierce thunderstorm, unperturbed by the bolts of lightning that struck the ground around him. He is also invoked against seasickness.

SAINT BONIFACE

Feast day: June 5. Archbishop of Mainz; apostle of Friesland and Germany

Attributes: A mitre, a staff

Saint Boniface was a highly regarded teacher, monk, and missionary. Originally named Winifreth (or Winfrid), Boniface was born in Devon, England, to landowning peasants. A pleasant, enthusiastic, and dedicated scholar, Boniface was educated by Benedictine monks and became a monk and schoolteacher himself. Boniface was the author of the first Latin grammar book to be written in England. By the time Boniface was thirty, he was a successful teacher and was ordained a priest. His popularity in England grew, and he was offered the position of abbot, but Boniface declined in order to become a missionary in the pagan-ridden Germanic lands of Friesland, Hesse, Thuringia (Hungary), and Bavaria. The saint

SAINT BONIFACE

made a pit stop in Rome on his journey and received a papal commission and his new name. Unable to make any headway with the Frieslanders, he admitted a rare defeat and returned to England. In 722, after another visit to Rome, he was made bishop and given a see at Mainz in 745.

As a missionary, he converted many and established Benedictine monasteries, schools, and churches in various regions throughout France and Germany. During one assembly before a group of potential Bavarian converts, Boniface vowed to defy the power of the pagan gods and struck down a giant oak tree sacred to the god of thunder, Thor. Many conversions occurred when no disaster ensued.

Boniface was also responsible for organizing and reforming the incorrigibly corrupt Church in France. He did so by dividing the area into provinces, each led by an archbishop in direct communication with Rome. In this manner, the pope was able to depose the last of the Frankish puppet-kings and place a friendly leader, Pepin, at the helm. Boniface presided over the new king's coronation in 751, a ceremony that was the origin of all subsequent coronations.

Always ambitious, Boniface returned to the site of his first defeat in Friesland in his late seventies. He was far more successful this time, managing to convert a significant number of people. However, the elderly saint was killed on the banks of the river Borne by a gang of renegade pagan bandits as he was readying himself to baptize more converts. The bandits graciously allowed Boniface to lay his head on his own Bible before they chopped it off.

SAINT NORBERT

TWELFTH CENTURY
SAINT NORBERT

Feast day: June 6. Founder of the Premonstratensian
Order (also called Norbertines)

Norbert was a swashbuckling youth who traveled the world in opulence and ease until he narrowly missed being struck by a lightning bolt during an intense thunderstorm. Scared out of his wits, Norbert thanked God for his life and, in gratitude, worked until he was ordained as a priest. He exchanged his wealth for poverty, giving away the profits from the sale of his grand estates to the poor. He preached in northern France and gained a vast reputation for eloquence and miracles. Once while saying Mass, a poisonous spider fell into the chalice of wine just as Norbert lifted it for blessing; rather than spill any of the Savior's blood, Norbert swallowed the wine in one gulp, spider and all, and survived unharmed.

Norbert started an austere order of monks, the Premonstratensians, who combined spiritual work with hard pastoral labor. He was a great proponent of clerical celibacy and a strict guardian of church property. His extreme views made him many enemies, some of whom were foiled in a plot to assassinate him.

TWELFTH CENTURY
SAINT ROBERT

Feast day: June 7

Accused of over-familiarity with a local woman, Robert of Newminster toiled to convince his fellow monks of his innocence. Saint Bernard, himself a victim of similar accusations, sent Robert a chastity belt in sympathy. The day Robert died, a friend had a vision of Robert's soul ascending to heaven in a ball of fire. Among the miracles attributed to this saint was that of a monk who fell off a ladder while whitewashing the monastery and walked away unscathed.

FOURTH CENTURY
Saint Alban

Feast day: June 21. The first martyr in Britain

Alban was a pagan soldier who sheltered a priest from persecution and was consequently converted and baptized. His former Christian-hounding colleagues, in pursuit of the priest, were sent to search Alban's house. Alban dressed himself in the priest's clothes to allow the older man to escape. The saint was arrested and condemned after refusing to give sacrifice to pagan gods.

At the death site—now known as the city of Saint Albans in England—one of the men chosen to execute him was converted instantly and refused to continue; the other managed to behead the saint, but his eyes fell out, an episode commonly depicted in art. The sick were often brought to Saint Alban's tomb for cure.

FIRST CENTURY
Saint Peter

Feast day: June 29, joint with Saint Paul. Leader of the apostles; patron of the Church and popes
Attributes: Keys, fish, ships, a rooster, chains, and an upside-down cross

Originally called Simon, and a fisherman by trade, Peter lived by the Sea of Galilee with his brother, Andrew, who introduced him to Jesus. Upon meeting the fisherman, Jesus called upon him to be a "fisher of men" and renamed him Peter. His baptismal name means "rock," alluding to the rock upon which the Christian Church would be built. Peter was married and took his wife with him on his journeys. He became a notable miracle worker and teacher, and the Gospel of Mark actually is attributed to him. Peter is the gatekeeper of heaven and the guardian of its keys; in art they are rendered as one silver key crossed against one gold key.

SAINT PETER

SAINT VERONICA

Peter was crucified under Nero, chained to his cross upside down. He is often painted as a square-faced man with curly hair and beard. His relics are buried under St. Peter's church in Rome.

JULY

FIRST CENTURY

SAINT VERONICA

Feast day: July 12. Represents one of the fourteen Stations of the Cross

Attribute: A veil

Veronica is the woman who supposedly wiped the face of Jesus when he stumbled under the weight of the cross on his way to Calvary. "Vera Icon," meaning "true image," may be the basis for her name, since the imprint of Jesus' visage was reportedly left on the cloth that Veronica used. A "veil of Veronica" has

been preserved at St. Peter's in Rome; it was highly revered during the Middle Ages. The Sixth Station of the Cross marks the site of her story, and she is always shown in art holding her veil.

ELEVENTH CENTURY

SAINT HENRY

Feast day: July 15. Holy Roman Emperor

Succeeding his father, Henry the Quarrelsome, as duke of Bavaria, Henry II was made emperor in 1002. Not above exerting his spiritual power, he used his alliance with the Church to further his goals of solidifying the German empire through war. Upon being crowned Holy Roman Emperor in 1014, Henry II reputedly restored wealth to many areas, although his creation of a cathedral and monastery in Bamberg helped to police citizenry as much as it helped to change their hearts. There is little temporal

SAINT HENRY

proof of Henry II's holiness, but the emperor claimed his lack of progeny was a result of a strict adherence to an ascetic lifestyle and an unconsummated marriage. He was canonized in 1146.

FIFTH CENTURY

SAINT ALEXIS

(ALSO CALLED ALEXIUS)

Feast day: July 17. Patron of beggars and the Alexian Brothers Nursing Society

Attributes: A palm, a scrip, a staff, and a stairwell

The dashing young son of a Roman patrician, Alexis became engaged to a wealthy woman after having secretly dedicated himself to the Church and chastity. Unwilling to disobey his parents, he married the woman but left, incorrupt, on their wedding night (with his bride's blessing) to embark on a long pilgrimage. For many years he lived as a beggar in Syria and gave whatever money he made to the poor. He returned to Rome years later, tattered, worn, and completely unrecognizable. Mistaken for a beggar even by his parents, he was permitted to live under the stairs outside his own house, a target for insult and the nightly slops.

After seventeen years, Alexis was found dying under the same stairs, clinging to a letter. That day, the pope was offering Mass for the emperor and his court when a holy voice told him to seek out the dying beggar. He did, and on finding him pried from the dead man's hand a letter that revealed his identity.

Alexis's remains were supposedly discovered with the relics of Saint Boniface when a church near Avertine Hill in Rome was being rebuilt in 1216. The church is now dedicated to both saints, and the wooden stairway under which Alexis lived in such torment is visible there.

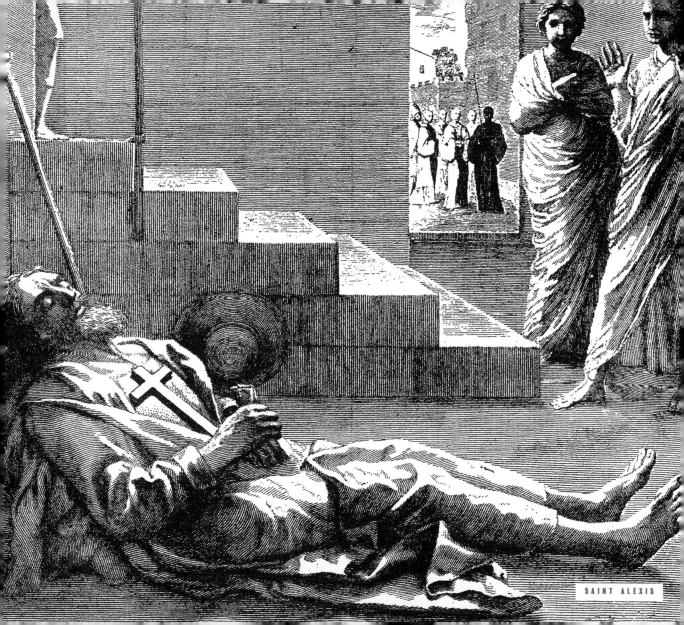

SAINT ALEXIS

DATES UNKNOWN

SAINT MARGARET OF ANTIOCH

(ALSO MARINA)

Feast day: July 20. Patroness of childbirth and the dying

Attribute: A dragon

The daughter of a pagan priest, Margaret was kidnapped by a Roman governor who tried to seduce her. When she refused, he had her arrested as a Christian. She was tortured in various appalling ways, perhaps the most fanciful of which was being swallowed by the devil in the guise of a dragon, who then burst apart, leaving her undigested and quite alive. Margaret swore that those who invoked her name or wrote or read her history would receive a crown in heaven. Those who called to her at their death beds would receive divine protection from evil; those who honored her with candles or in churches would get anything they prayed for; and pregnant women who venerate her would escape the dangers of childbirth. She is often shown in art lancing a dragon or emerging from one.

DATES UNKNOWN

SAINT WILGEFORTIS

(ALSO CALLED UNCUMBER AND LIBERATA)

Feast day: July 20

According to legend, Wilgefortis was a septuplet born to the queen of Portugal (who had nine children). Initially pagan, Wilgefortis and her brothers and sisters all became Christian and were martyred. When Wilgefortis's father insisted she marry a Sicilian prince, the girl knelt down and prayed that she would be made so unattractive that the prince

SAINT MARGARET OF ANTIOCH

would not want her. In due time, a bushy beard and mustache sprouted on her face, and her prayers were answered: her suitor would have nothing to do with her. Her father, enraged and disgusted, had her crucified.

Wilgefortis swore on her last breath that all who prayed to her would be freed of their weighty troubles. Taking the saint at her word, in England she is often called Uncumber because, as legend has it, she will rid women of their irksome husbands for a peck of oats.

Wilgefortis's legend may have derived from the fact that in the Middle Ages ancient vested crucifixes were mistaken for bearded women.

THIRD CENTURY

SAINT CHRISTINA

Feast day: July 24

Attribute: A millstone

A virgin whose cult enjoyed great popularity in the Middle Ages, Christina was a tempestuous teenager when, in a fit of adolescent rebellion, she threw all of her family's precious idols to the floor, smashing them to bits. She then gave their entire hoard of gold and silver pieces to the poor behind her parents' back.

Christina was imprisoned and sentenced to death by being cast into a lake with a millstone around her neck—her parents did not object. She survived only to endure a burning and further torture with a knife and tongs. Eventually the young girl was killed by being shot with three arrows. She often appears in art with Saint Ursula and has been painted by Veronese and Cranach.

FIRST CENTURY

SAINT CHRISTOPHER

Feast day: July 25. One of the Fourteen Holy Helpers;
patron of travelers and motorists
Attributes: A river, a flowering staff, an arrow,
a dog's head

Christopher was a massive man, who, because of his great strength, wished to work for the greatest king on earth. This desire initially led him to seek out the devil. In the midst of his search for this most powerful king, he met a mysterious hermit who instructed him to stand on the edge of a swollen river, swift with a sharp undercurrent, and aid travelers in crossing. He did so, and on one especially stormy night he encountered a child there. This child climbed on his back and they began to cross; as Christopher walked through the water, the current grew stronger and the child heavier with each step. He persevered and eventually reached the other side, where the child revealed himself to be Jesus. The child proclaimed to Christopher (whose name means Christ-bearer) that he had just borne the weight of the one who had created the entire world. He instructed Christopher to plant his staff outside his hut, and the following day the stick turned into a palm tree bearing fruits and flowers, proving to the giant the truth of what had taken place.

Christopher was baptized and taken prisoner soon afterward when he refused to recant his new faith. Two prostitutes were sent to defile him, and he was beaten with iron rods and shot at with arrows (all of which missed him, except for one that ricocheted off his skin and into the king's eye). Finally, he was beheaded. As Christopher died, he prayed that all who saw him and had faith would be saved from fire, storm, and earthquake.

In the Middle Ages, Christopher's figure reportedly stood guard at the south door of the church in almost every parish, so that each person would see him immediately upon entering. It is believed that one who sees Saint Christopher's image will be protected throughout the day from disaster and sudden death. Christopher's cult has grown in popularity as motor and air travel have increased. His image is often incorporated into travel-related emblems and badges. Paintings usually depict him, with and without a dog's head (it was believed that he begged the Lord to make him as ugly as a dog to escape the attentions of female admirers), carrying Jesus as a child and surrounded by the two prostitutes (sometimes envisioned as sexy mermaids), the hermit, the river, his flowering staff, boats, fish, and the arrow wounding the king.

FIRST CENTURY

SAINT ANNE

(ALSO CALLED ANN, ANNA, SUSANNA(H), AND HANNAH)

Feast day: July 26. Patroness of housewives and cabinet makers

Attribute: A book

Mother of the Virgin Mary, Anne is the symbol of perfect motherhood. Infertile for twenty years, she was a wealthy woman living in Bethlehem and married to a man named Joachim (a saint in his own right). Joachim was excluded from the local temple because he did not have a son, and so he turned, in sorrow, to the lonely life of shepherding.

Bereft and despairing over her husband, one day Anne put on her wedding gown and went to rest in her garden. As she sat, she jealously watched a sparrow feed its

SAINT JOACHIM AND SAINT ANNE

young and prayed fervently that she could do the same. Miraculously, an angel appeared and told Anne to run to the Golden Gate (the gates of Jerusalem) and meet her husband returning from the fields. She greeted Joachim with a kiss and instantly, immaculately, conceived Mary, whom she dedicated to God on the spot. Anne is often featured in images of the family circle with Jesus and Mary; in some versions, she is teaching Mary to read.

FOURTH CENTURY

SAINT PANTALEON

Feast day: July 27. One of the Fourteen Holy Helpers
Attribute: An olive tree.

Saint Pantaleon, whose name means "all merciful," was a doctor who was born Christian and went to practice for Emperor Galerius. Led astray by the luxurious pagan festivities and carefree atti-

tudes of the court, Pantaleon forgot his faith for a while, only to reaffirm his commitment during the Diocletian persecutions of the Christians. He then took to healing the sick and needy for free. His fellow doctors denounced him as a Christian, and Pantaleon was arrested and beheaded at the foot of a barren olive tree. The tree burst into bloom the moment his blood seeped into its roots.

A vial of Pantaleon's blood (although it was believed that milk, rather than blood, flowed from the saint's veins) has been preserved in the cathedral at Ravello, Italy. Once a year, on his feast day, the dried blood in the vial liquefies and turns a brilliant shade of red, according to the many witnesses who tell of this phenomenon. His relics lie in the church of St. Denys in Paris. Pantaleon was widely venerated in the Middle Ages, and it was believed he could cure people of demonic possession and wasting diseases. He is one of the most popular saints in Greece, Russia, the Near East, and North Africa.

THIRD CENTURY
SEVEN SLEEPERS OF EPHESUS

Feast day: July 27

Seven young noblemen were run out of town for their Christian faith by Emperor Decius. They hid in a cave that the emperor walled up. Instead of suffocating, the men fell asleep. One hundred years later, a local businessman began removing stones from the exterior of the cave to use in his construction site. The noise stirred the seven men, and they woke up to a world that was completely different. Causing suspicion by the funny way they were dressed and their outdated coins, the seven men were brought before the police. They brought the authorities back to their cave and were released. The young men went back to sleep and have not wakened to this day. The story *Rip Van Winkle* has its origin in this legend, which supports the belief in resurrection.

FIRST CENTURY
SAINT MARTHA

Feast day: July 29. Patroness of cooks and housekeepers
Attributes: A ladle, keys, and a broom

Martha has gone down in history as the original cranky housewife. She was sister to Lazarus and

SAINT MARTHA

Mary Magdalene, and thus she had the honor of entertaining Jesus when he visited, according to the Gospel of John. On one such night, Jesus was impelled to chastise Martha for her persistent griping about her sister: Mary did not help enough with the housework, preferring instead to sit idle and listen to Jesus' teachings. This scolding has been interpreted as Jesus justifying the value of a contemplative life over that of an active life. Martha was chastened.

In due time, Martha and her siblings were forced to sail from their home to avoid persecution. They set to sea in a leaky boat that ended up in the Rhône, where they disembarked and promptly began to convert the region of France around Marseilles. In Provence, Martha rid the area of a pesky and ferocious dragon by sprinkling holy water over its back and leading it away with her sash.

SIXTEENTH CENTURY

SAINT IGNATIUS

Feast day: July 31. Founder of the Jesuits;
patron of spiritual exercises and retreats, as well as
many schools and colleges.
Attributes: a Jesuit habit and the monogram IHS

The son of a Basque nobleman, Ignatius was a soldier who fought and was wounded in the siege of Pamplona. During his recovery, he asked for books about knights and romance but was given instead devotional readings that changed his life. He decided to turn away from his violent career and follow God. His leg, injured by a cannonball, never healed properly, and he was destined to walk with a pronounced limp the rest of his life. Despite this deformity, Ignatius managed a pilgrimage to Jerusalem, where he began to conceive of his new order, the Society of

S. IGNATIUS. THEOPH.

B.IGNATIVS LOYOLA FVNDATOR Soc. IESV.

Jesus. Ignatius went to Spain where, although he was in his thirties, he studied with little schoolchildren to make up for holes in his education. He returned to Paris, gathering six disciples to help him carry out his new order's program: education, obedience, and missionary work in faraway lands. The Society of Jesus quickly grew from seven to ten to sixty to one thousand, and soon flourished throughout Europe. Ignatius also established houses in Rome for fallen women and converted Jews. His position has been compared to that of a general in God's army, and the loyalty expected from its members to that of a military commitment. The Jesuits were particularly keen proponents of the Spanish Inquisition.

Saint Ignatius is portrayed in art dressed in the black robe, tonsure, and high collar of the Jesuits, the monogram IHS (adopted by the order) inscribed on his chest or on a book that he carries. Occasionally he may tread on a dragon symbolizing his victory over the devil. Jesuit schools, colleges, and churches call him patron.

AUGUST

SECOND CENTURY

SAINTS FAITH, HOPE, AND CHARITY

Feast day: August 1. The three theological virtues

These three girls, whose Greek names are, respectively, Pistis, Elpis, and Agape, were the Roman daughters of Sophia (Wisdom) who were put to death during the reign of Emperor Hadrian. They were twelve, ten, and nine years old.

SAINT LAURENCE

FOURTH CENTURY
SAINT AFRA

Feast day: August 5

A disreputable courtesan who ran a brothel in Augsburg, Germany, Afra sheltered a priest running away from the police. During his brief stay, the priest, named Narcissus, managed to convert not only Afra but her mother and three of her prostitutes as well. Afra was able to save the man who saved her soul, but she and the other women were burnt at the stake.

THIRD CENTURY
SAINT LAURENCE

Feast day: August 10. Patron of the poor
Attributes: A gridiron, a long cross

A well-known Spanish deacon who was close to Pope Sixtus II, Laurence was known for his miraculous cures and his humility; he often washed the feet of persecuted Christians in Rome. After the martyrdom of Pope Sixtus II, Laurence (who was in charge of the Church's records and books) refused to hand over the Church's estate to the authorities, and instead gave it away to the poor. For this, he was scourged and roasted on a gridiron.

Remarkably, he was reputed to have said to his executioner halfway through the grisly deed: "You have cooked me through on one side, turn me over so that you may eat me well done."

When his tomb was opened four hundred years later to admit the corpse of Saint Stephen, Laurence moved over and gave his hand to his companion; hence he became known as "the courteous Spaniard." In art, he often carries a long cross and walks toward a fire or is shown with the gridiron. Laurence can free one soul from Purgatory every Friday.

THIRD CENTURY

SAINT ALEXANDER

Feast day: August 11

Of several saints named Alexander, this one was a charcoal burner chosen by Saint Gregory to be bishop of a town on the Black Sea. Although Alexander was seemingly underqualified for the job, Saint Gregory admired the sooty face and blackened hands of the charcoal burner more than the smooth skin of other more nobly born candidates. Bishop Alexander was said to possess wisdom and strength and was eventually burnt at the stake.

THIRTEENTH CENTURY

SAINT CLARE

(ALSO CALLED CLARA, CLAIRE)

Feast day: August 12. Founder of the Poor Clares; patroness of television

Attribute: A monstrance or "pyx"

The eighteen-year-old Clare, a native of Assisi, was so moved by a sermon given by Saint Francis that she renounced all her possessions and her family, snuck out of her house by the door reserved for corpses, joined Francis at his monastery — where he cut off all

SAINT CLARE

her hair — and began her life as a nun. She attained the position of abbess of a house near the church of San Damiano in Assisi that lived in strict adherence to the rule of Saint Francis. The life was extremely simple; the women lived in grave poverty and survived entirely off alms. Despite the austerity, Clare's order grew and spread into other parts of Europe. When Saint Francis died, he asked that his body be carried back to Assisi via Clare's house. There, the women received his body and gently bathed its feet.

A nurturing woman with a great love of nature, Clare ran her nunnery with great delight, caring for her fellow sisters, tending its gardens, sewing altar cloths, and graciously refusing material help in her rigid commitment to a life of abject poverty. The last twenty-five years of her life were wracked by illness, but nevertheless Clare was able to turn back the marauding troops of Emperor Frederick II at the gates of Assisi in 1244 by displaying a vessel holding the Eucharist.

THIRD CENTURY

SAINT HIPPOLYTUS

Feast day: August 13. Patron of horses

Attribute: A horse

According to legend, there are two martyrs named Hippolytus (meaning "loosed horse"), and their identities are often confused. One man was an early and important writer in Italy who opposed the Roman bishops and was exiled to Sardinia during the reign of Emperor Maximinus.

The other Hippolytus, of which little verifiable information is known, was allegedly a jailer of Saint Laurence and was converted by the exemplary behavior of his prisoner. When Laurence was put to death, Hippolytus buried the body in grief and revealed his new faith to his superiors. He was swiftly condemned and was either roped to a wild horse who dragged him to his end or was bound by his limbs to wild horses who tore him apart like

SAINT HIPPOLYTUS

Theseus's son Hippolytus in Greek history. Nineteen members of his family and his nurse were also martyred. In England, sick horses were often brought to his shrine for cure.

SIXTH CENTURY

SAINT ARMEL

Feast day: August 16. Welsh abbot, founded monasteries at Plouarmel and Ploermel; common patron of hospitals
Attribute: a dragon with yoke

The legend of Saint Armel claims that this Welshman disposed of a dragon by leading it to Mont-Saint-Armel and ordering it to dive into the depths of the river below. His cult spread during the Middle Ages from Brittany to England, supported by Henry VII, who claimed that his ship was saved from disaster off the coast of Brittany by Armel's intervention. There is a statue of Armel in the King's Chapel at

Westminster Abbey. Armel is generally seen in art clad in armor, leading a dragon with a yoke around its neck. He is invoked to cure headaches, fever, gout, colic, and rheumatism.

FOURTEENTH CENTURY

SAINT ROCH

(ALSO CALLED ROCK)

Feast day: August 17. Patron of invalids, invoked against the plague

Attribute: A dog

Born in Montpellier, France, Roch had wealthy parents who died when he was twenty, leaving him a rich man. He converted to a religious life and gave all his money away to hospitals and for support of the poor. On a pilgrimage to Rome, when the plague was just beginning to reach epidemic proportions, he took to living as a hermit and became a healer to the plague-stricken. He was infected by the plague (represented in art as a red, infected sore on his leg) and would have died if not for a faithful dog who brought him food every day.

When Roch came back to Montpellier, he was so ravaged by poverty and disease that his own uncle refused to recognize him, and he was thrown into jail as a spy. He spent five years in a dungeon, comforted

SAINT ROCH

by an angel. While in jail he wrote a history of his life, which combined with a particular birthmark, proved his identity after his death. Repentant, his family reburied his body with honor. Saint Roch is invoked as protection against the plague, cholera, and all other infectious diseases. His cult became especially popular in the nineteenth century with a massive outbreak of cholera.

FOURTH CENTURY

Saint Helena

Feast day: August 18

Attributes: A cross carried by angels and the instruments of the Passion

Of humble birth, Helena became the most powerful woman in the world when she married the emperor Constantius. As empress, she bore him one son, who became Constantine the Great, but she was divorced by Constantius twenty years later because of her lowly birth. Originally an enemy of Christianity, Helena was converted at the age of sixty-three, at the urging of her son. When Constantine was made emperor, he declared Christianity a tolerated religion and Helena used her wealth and prestige to spread her faith. When Helena was in her eighties she made a pilgrimage to the Holy Land in search of the Cross. She was wonderfully successful, finding not only the Cross, but the seamless coat Christ wore on his journey, and the nails (some accounts describe them as being gold) of the Crucifixion. Thus she is always depicted in art either carrying or dreaming of the Cross, the coat, or the nails. One of the pillars supporting the dome of St. Peter's in Rome is dedicated to Saint Helena, and there is a statue of her nearby.

SAINT BERNARD

TWELFTH CENTURY

SAINT BERNARD

Feast day: August 20. One of the Doctors of the Church;
founder of the Cistercian Order

Attributes: A beehive, a chained devil

Bernard's mother dreamed of a big white dog with a black back the night her son was born. This foretold that Bernard would become a monk and wear the white tunic and black scapular of the Benedictine order at Citeaux. Bernard renounced the world at an early age, and his reasoning and person were so persuasive that he inspired his uncle and twenty-nine other relatives and friends to do the same. As a young man, he studied at the University of Paris, and then he duly followed his birth-prophecy and entered into the poverty-stricken order in his early twenties.

In his youth, Bernard was consistently tormented by fleshly desire at the sight of beautiful women and would throw himself into the nearest pond, some half-frozen, to promote resistance. This victory over temptation is often celebrated in art by the image of a devil chained at Bernard's feet as he writes or preaches.

In time, Bernard channeled his passion to become a vehement and eloquent speaker who drew crowds of followers with his honeyed voice (hence his emblem), and he earned a reputation as "the mellifluous doctor." According to legend, the Virgin Mary once appeared to Bernard during an excruciating period of writer's block. In pity, she moistened the monk's lips with milk from her own breast so that his words would be irresistible.

Bernard rose swiftly and soon established his own order with twenty-five fellow monks at Clairvaux in the Valley of Wormwood in Aube. In his initial gust of enthusiasm, he was an overly severe abbot, often starving his brood by feeding them parsimonious bits of barley bread. He mended his ways and was soon regarded as the most popular mouthpiece of Christianity in Europe. Clairvaux, in turn, became very successful, spawning other houses and boosting its own fellowship to seven hundred by the time Bernard died. Bernard is considered one of the most influential, charismatic, and controversial personalities of his time.

Bernard was also known to be a stubborn and opinionated man who made many enemies. His biggest failure took place during the Second Crusade, for which he drummed up rabid enthusiasm, allying a military conquest with his own beliefs. Many people rallied to his call and took up the cross; when the Second Crusade dissolved into random pillage and looting, many blamed Bernard. Despite this, Bernard was a powerful force during his lifetime, and he served an essential role in twelfth-century Church reform.

THIRTEENTH CENTURY

Saint Louis of France

(Louis IX)

Feast day: August 25. King of France (1226–1270);
patron of France and the French monarchy
Attribute: A royal crown and a robe embroidered with
fleur-de-lis, the symbol of French royalty

Leader of the Seventh Crusade, Louis was defeated at El Mansura and ransomed. He and his son later undertook the Eighth Crusade, during which he was taken prisoner in Tunis and died of typhoid fever. He ruled over France during a great period of enlightenment, when universities were built and intellectual developments were encouraged. He was a wise and patient king, prominent in almsgiving and justice, who forbade foul and blasphemous language.

King Louis IX brought to France, among the spoils of war, the crown of thorns. He built the

cathedral of Sainte-Chapelle, allegedly using the three nails taken from the cross, specifically to house and honor the precious object. Artists commonly render him carrying the crown of thorns and the three nails.

SAINT JOHN THE BAPTIST

Feast day: August 29 (beheading) and June 24 (nativity)

Attributes: Wings, a lamb, a honey pot

John the Baptist, the son of Saint Elizabeth and Saint Zachary, is the most direct predecessor of Jesus. Elizabeth was supposed to be past child-bearing age when she miraculously conceived. A close relative to Jesus (Elizabeth was Mary's cousin), John was a prophet who lived as a hermit in the desert eating locusts and dressing in camel cloth. He be-

came a strident preacher, demanding repentance of sins and baptism in a body of water as the sign of a redeemed soul. His voice was the one "crying in the wilderness," and he prophesied that someday there would come a man who would be greater than he and the savior of humanity. John's principal role in history is that he baptized Jesus and thereby indicated to the world the fulfiller of his prophecy.

John the Baptist was imprisoned for denouncing the incestuous marriage of Herod Antipas, one of the rulers of Palestine. Antipas had married his niece, Herodias, who also happened to be another brother's wife. Salome, Herodias's daughter, had danced and entertained her stepfather/great-uncle to the man's utter delight. In return, he told the girl she might have anything she wished. Spurred on by her mother, Salome bewitchingly replied that she would like the head of John the Baptist on a plate. Executioners were promptly dispatched, and in due time, the head was brought forth. Salome victoriously presented it to her mother. John's disciples were permitted to bury his body.

John is most frequently represented in art baptizing Jesus. Dressed in camel hair, he might carry a cross with a long handle and be accompanied by a lamb. The saint is also often depicted in images of the Holy Family as a child sitting with Jesus at Mary's knee.

SAINT ROSE OF LIMA

Feast day: August 30. Patroness of South America and the Philippines

The first American saint, Rose was born in Lima, Peru, and lived there her entire thirty-one years. An astonishing natural beauty, Rose went to great length to ruin her looks: rubbing pepper on her face to cause a blotchy complexion; dipping her smooth, soft hands into lime; and, on one occasion, pushing a pin into her head. In addition, she deprived herself of food, drink, and sleep on a regular basis and became a Dominican nun. When her parents were bankrupted by speculating in the mining business, Rose went to work sewing and laboring in the garden. She lived the latter part of her life as a recluse in a small hut in her garden, dying of an illness that was appar-

SAINT ROSE OF LIMA

ently caused by her severe mental and physical habits. She is often shown wearing a garland of roses.

SEPTEMBER

SEVENTH CENTURY

SAINT FIACRE

Feast day: September 1. Patron of gardeners

Attribute: A spade

An Irish missionary who settled on the banks of the Marne in Normandy (a spot later known as La Brie, where his shrine is located), Fiacre was granted by the local bishop enough land for his community as he could dig in one day. He managed to unearth quite a parcel, and many pilgrims came to him to bask in his wisdom and generosity. He was a great cultivator, both of the earth and of souls, and after his

death he became a beloved saint to royalty and commoners, answering many prayers with his favors. His cult flourished in France, peaking in the mid-seventeenth century. During this time, cabs used to gather outside the Hotel Saint-Fiacre in Paris and for this reason, the word *fiacre* has come to mean "taxi" or "cab" in French.

SIXTH CENTURY

SAINT GILES

Feast day: September 1. One of the Fourteen Holy Helpers; patron of the handicapped, nursing mothers, blacksmiths, and lepers

Attributes: A deer and an arrow

Giles was an Athenian who became a hermit in the forest at Nîmes, France. His only friend was a deer who had taken refuge with him. One day, while out hunting in the forest, the king shot an arrow at the deer and missed, hitting Giles's leg instead. Wounded and crippled, Giles graciously forgave the king, who was so relieved he authorized Giles to found a monastery in Provence (St. Giles).

An enormously popular saint in the Middle Ages, Giles was invoked to aid in a range of afflictions: epilepsy, insanity, sterility, and fear of confession—Giles supposedly had the ability to absolve someone's sin even if he or she could not bear to say it out loud. Giles's name is associated with hospitals and blacksmiths as his churches were often positioned at crossroads where people could rest while their horses were being shod at blacksmith shops nearby.

FOURTH CENTURY

SAINT PAPHNUTIUS

Feast day: September 11

Attributes: A palm tree, a musician

Paphnutius was a bishop in Alexandria who lived in the desert. He was persecuted, but survived, under Emperor Maximinus. While praying one day, he asked for some sort of indication of his worth to God. For an answer he was directed toward a street musician, whom Paphnutius recognized to be his equal in the eyes of God. Paphnutius was opposed to clerical celibacy, though he was himself celibate. His attribute is a palm tree.

TENTH CENTURY

Saint Edith

Feast day: September 16

The daughter of King Edgar and his concubine, Wilfrida, who happened to be a novice at Wilton Abbey, Kent, Edith was raised in her mother's convent and became, naturally, keen on pursuing a religious life. Her father wanted to show her a world outside the convent walls, but she was adamant in her refusal never to set foot outside the abbey. Refusing again and again the possibilities afforded her as the king's daughter, Edith was content in her cloister, although she reportedly had a penchant for dressing in fancy clothes.

SEVENTEENTH CENTURY

Saint Joseph of Cupertino

Feast day: September 18

Born in Brindisi, Italy, to poor parents, Saint Joseph of Cupertino was an overweight, dim-witted youth whose parents, for lack of anything better to do with him, apprenticed the boy to a shoemaker. The shoemaker nicknamed Joseph "the Gaper" for his constant wide-eyed and slack-jawed expression. Failing at his apprenticeship, Joseph became a stable boy for the local Franciscan monastery and slowly worked to gain admittance into the brotherhood. He was ordained and lived simply, often experiencing states of ecstasy in which he would have many visions and levitate. He was once seen floating in through the church door and over the heads of the worshipers, finally coming to roost on the altar. In another flight, he floated up into an olive tree and sat on a branch, beaming at the onlookers below.

SAINT JOSEPH

SAINT EUSTACE

Joseph was said to be an open-hearted, kind individual who healed and aided many people. He was legendary for his ability to recognize sinners, whose faces appeared black to him, and to sniff out perverts and sex offenders by their noxious odor.

Often dealt with severely by his fellow Franciscans for his outrageous (and theatrical) tendencies, Joseph endured his frequent punishments and exile with his characteristic patience and good nature.

FOURTH CENTURY
SAINT JANUARIUS

Feast day: September 19. Patron of Naples

Saint Januarius was the bishop of Benevento persecuted under Emperor Diocletian. Upon hearing of four imprisoned Christians headed for the games in the arena, Januarius paid them a visit and was arrested as well. All five were thrown to the

savage beasts in front of giddy spectators, but none of the beasts would touch the Christians. Januarius was then beheaded. A woman filled two ampoules with his blood at his execution, and they now reside on the chapel altar of the cathedral in Naples. Like the blood of Saint Pantaleon, the blood in the ampoules is known to liquefy eighteen times a year. Saint Januarius is credited with saving the city of Naples when Mount Vesuvius threatened to erupt.

DATES UNKNOWN
SAINT EUSTACE

Feast day: September 20. One of the Fourteen Holy Helpers; patron of hunters,
Attribute: A stag

A commanding general in the Roman army named Placidas loved the thrill of the hunt. While on leave from his duties, Placidas forayed into the wilderness as he was wont to do and came upon a beautiful white stag, between whose magnificent antlers hung a crucifix. The tiny figure hanging on the cross spoke to Placidas, warning him of many misfortunes that would come to pass. Taken aback by the beauty and wonder of the sight, Placidas instantly converted and changed his name to Eustace. Despite his conversion, bad things did indeed happen to the saint: pirates carried off his wife; a wolf made off with one child, and a lion with the other. Luckily, all three managed to escape, but they did not reunite with Eustace for fifteen years. When they were finally brought together by the local authorities to make grateful sacrifice to pagan gods, the family refused and were martyred by being stuffed inside a bronze bull and roasted.

THIRD CENTURY

SAINT MAURICE AND COMPANIONS

Feast day: September 22. Patron of Austria, Piedmont, Savoy, and Sardinia

Attributes: An ax, a martyr's crown; an eagle near him or on his banner represents the eagle of Austria

One of the soldier saints, Maurice commanded a legion of 6,600 Theban men in the Roman army, all recruited in Egypt. When the emperor Maximian, trying to ensure a military success in Gaul, ordered all of his troops to sacrifice to pagan gods, they refused and withdrew to what was then called Agenaum. As punishment, the emperor ordered that every tenth man be beheaded until his original command was obeyed. The entire army persistently refused until every man was killed. Maurice stood among his troops mustering their courage until it was his turn, and then he benignly lay his head upon a

St. Maurice

stone, joining his men in death. The stone can still be seen, in the town now called Saint Moritz (or Saint-Maurice-en-Valais), Switzerland. Maurice is also invoked by weavers, dyers, and soldiers, in particular, the Papal Swiss Guards.

FIRST CENTURY

SAINT THECLA

Feast day: September 23

Thecla was a maiden who, upon her conversion to Christianity by Saint Paul, broke off her engagement to a popular young man. Her parents had Paul exiled; Thecla was doomed to be burned at the stake. While she was on the pyre, a sudden storm blew in and doused the flames. Thecla was then sent into the coliseum where she was to be eaten by lions and bears. She baptized herself in a ditch on the sidelines, and the animals refused to eat her. She then escaped wear-

ing men's clothes and joined Paul to preach.

Thecla lived in a cave and spread her faith for the next seventy-two years, and she became known for her miracle working. One time, a gang of men was sent to ravish and kill her. Spotting them coming, the virgin furiously prayed for salvation, and, wondrously, the rocks below her feet opened and swallowed her into the safety of the earth.

FOURTH CENTURY

SAINTS CYPRIAN AND JUSTINA

Feast day: September 26

Attribute: A unicorn

Cyprian was a sorcerer hired by a pagan nobleman to aid his efforts to deflower the virgin Justina. Cyprian went to great lengths, using every magic spell he knew—even selling his soul to the devil—

to accomplish the deed, filling the poor girl's head with lustful visions and conjuring up the devil himself to tempt her. He failed, nevertheless, and fell into a deep depression.

Justina took pity on Cyprian and converted him. She became an abbess and he a bishop, but both were later beheaded. The unicorn symbolizes Justina's incorruptible purity.

DATES UNKNOWN

SAINTS COSMAS AND DAMIAN

Feast day: September 27. Patrons of doctors

and the Medicis

Attributes: A doctor's gown and various medical instruments

Twin brothers and doctors, Cosmas and Damian practiced for free and were said to have divine skill in healing both animals and men. In the most pic-

turesque incident recorded they grafted a black leg onto the cancerous, live body of a white man. They were tirelessly persecuted and suffered many horrors: Cast into the sea in Syria, they were rescued by angels; thrown into a bonfire, they emerged unscorched as the flames from the pyre turned on their executioners; when stoned, the stones rebounded off them and hit their accusers instead; finally, they were simply beheaded.

The intercession of Cosmas and Damian has been the cause of many miraculous cures. Often a sick person was told to sleep in one of their churches, where he or she would be visited by dreams that would reveal the cure. They are also called upon to avert plagues and epidemics.

In art the brothers always appear in the long red gowns of doctors with a box of ointment, a pestle, a mortar, surgical instruments, and, occasionally urine in a flask. During the Renaissance, their cult was encouraged and patronized by the Medicis—a number of whom were called Cosimo—which accounts for how often the saintly pair were depicted in paintings of that era. Michelangelo sculpted their images for the Medici Chapel in Florence.

SAINT WENCESLAUS

Feast day: September 28. Patron of Czechoslovakia

Attribute: A dagger

The subject of the popular Christmas carol "Good King Wenceslaus," this saint lived in Bohemia, becoming king after his father was killed. Wenceslaus was brought up as a Christian by his grandmother, but his mother and brother, Boleslaus, were sworn enemies to his faith. Once king, Wenceslaus forged a pact with Germany that preserved peace and Christianity in his country by recognizing the German emperor, Henry I, to be his overlord. Boleslaus, a rabble-rouser with no hope for succession (Wenceslaus had a son), accused his brother of sacrificing Bohemia's sovereignty and secretly organized an opposition. The evil Boleslaus invited the king to keep the feast of Saints Cosmas and Damian with him the next day. As Wenceslaus trustingly walked to church the following morning he was sabotaged and killed by Boleslaus and his friends. The "good king" died on the church steps, asking pardon for his brother's deed.

The lyrics to "Good King Wenceslaus" were penned in the nineteenth century by J. M. Neale, commemorating the story that King Wenceslaus would often trudge through bitterly cold nights carrying logs for a poor man's fire. His attendant was able to keep up with the king by stepping in the saint's deep footprints made in the snow. The Crown of Wenceslaus is a symbol of Czech nationalism.

Saint Michael the Archangel

Feast day: September 29, Michaelmas. First of the seven archangels and the leader of the hosts of heaven; protector of high places; patron of cemeteries and mountain tops

Attributes: Armor and wings, a scale

The archangel Michael routed Lucifer when Lucifer rebelled against God and his divine order; Michael physically cast him from the heavens into the fiery pits of hell. Often depicted as a winged soldier in armor because he fights against evil, Michael also rescues souls from hell, leading them up to heaven. His feast day, known in Britain as Michaelmas, coincides with the migration of geese, the original source of the traditional Michaelmas goose dinner. In art, he is often pictured in full armor slaying evil in the form of the devil or a dragon or holding the heavenly scales and weighing souls. His most famous chapel is on Mont-Saint-Michel in Normandy.

FIFTH CENTURY

Saint Jerome

Feast day: September 30. Doctor of the Church; patron of librarians

Attributes: A lion and a stone

SAINT JEROME

Author of the first Latin edition of the Bible (the Vulgate, the official version of the Church of Rome), Jerome was a brilliant if cantankerous scholar. A student of Greek, Latin, and Hebrew, Jerome was baptized at age eighteen after a vision in which God appeared and scolded him for not being a Christian. Though he became a fully ordained priest, Jerome never said

SAN JERONIMO

Mass, preferring to retreat to the desert with his books and letters. After four years in the desert, he was called back to Rome to translate the Bible, and during this period he attracted a bevy of widows (among them Saint Paula) who were living together in monastic style. He instructed and accompanied the women often, an association that spawned suspicious rumors and quarrels over Jerome's celibacy. In truth, Jerome had suffered violent temptations of the flesh while in the desert, once envisioning a band of naked maidens cavorting around him. He threw himself upon his crucifix in retaliation and beat his breast with a nearby stone.

Never a particularly convivial man, Jerome was prone to tantrums and could be brutal with his wit and pen. As a result he made many enemies and fought with almost everyone. Greatly respected for his enormous intellect, it was widely believed that had it not been for the episode with the stone, Jerome would never have been made a saint. He is often por-

S. REMY   LA ROYNE CLOTILDE   LE·ROY·CLOVIS

Clotilde Royne a saint Remy envoye
Diligemment pour le coeur emouvoir
Du roy clovis afin qui le pourvoye
De saincte foy quon chacu doibt amour

trayed in art beating himself with the stone or writing at his desk, accompanied by a lion and wearing a cardinal's hat. The lion was tamed by Jerome when he pulled a thorn from its paw. Infrequently, Jerome is shown listening to the call of a trumpet.

OCTOBER

SIXTH CENTURY
SAINT REMÍ
(ALSO CALLED REMIGIUS)

Feast day: October 1

Attribute: A dove

Bishop of Rheims, Saint Remí baptized and anointed Clovis as king of the Franks; a dove brought him the vial of holy oil and is thus pictured with Remí in art. He was credited with filling an empty barrel with wine and stopping a fire that threatened the city of Rheims just by raising his hand. He was single-handedly responsible for converting thousands of Franks who followed their king into Christianity. It is widely believed that Remí was seven feet tall. His cathedral stands in Rheims.

NINETEENTH CENTURY
SAINT THÉRÈSE

Feast day: October 3

Attribute. A bouquet of roses

One of the most popular saints in modern times. Thérèse was a young girl of fifteen when she joined the Carmelite order of nuns in Lisieux, already convinced that she would be a saint. Initially given menial tasks of washing, ironing, and cleaning, Thérèse eventually became the mistress of the novices in the convent. A quiet and, during her

SAINT THÉRÈSE

lifetime, unremarkable nun, Thérèse suffered severe bouts of depression and neurosis that she took pains to hide in her endless striving for perfection and selfless love. Deathly ill with tuberculosis, Thérèse promised upon her death to loose a shower of roses in the form of favors and miracles from heaven. At the moment of her departure at age twenty-three, a fellow sister ran outside to gaze up at what was an overcast sky. Distraught, the nun asked why there might not be stars in the heavens to commemorate such a passing. Before her eyes, the clouds parted and revealed a hood of twinkling stars. This occurrence was the first of many miracles, cures, conversions, and favors granted following the death of Thérèse. Her Carmelite mother superior and sister, Agnes, edited and published Saint Thérèse's autobiography, *The Story of a Soul*, which tells of the sweetness and simplicity with which Thérèse approached her duties.

Terese of Avila, the patron saint of Spain (feast day: October 15), was a Carmelite nun in the sixteenth century. A writer, reformer, and much-respected speaker, Terese spent the early part of her life as a typical teenager, interested primarily in clothes and romance. Her father sent her away to be educated by nuns, and she later took the veil and experienced violent transports and visions, which inspired a number of painters and sculptors. The convent she established, St. Joseph of Avila, was based on the rules of strict enclosure, poverty, and solitary prayer. In 1970, she was declared a Doctor of the Church, the first female saint to receive this honor. Terese of Avila is frequently depicted in art with a flaming arrow or a dove above her head. There is a famous sculpture of her by Bernini located in the church of St. Maria della Vittoria in Rome.

Poissons, mes frères, benissez le Seigneur tout Puissant

THIRTEENTH CENTURY

SAINT FRANCIS OF ASSISI

Feast day: October 4. Founder of the Franciscan order;
patron of animals, birds, and environmentalists
Attributes: The Franciscan brown cloak with cord
belt and animals, marks of the stigmata

Originally christened John, or Giovanni, Francis's name was changed to Francesco (Frenchman) because of his mother's French heritage and the fact that he was christened just after his father returned from a successful business trip to France. Francis was a kind and simple boy who lived the luxurious life of a rich merchant's son until he was arrested during the wars between Assisi and Perugia. Surviving a perilous bout of illness

while imprisoned, Francis was further humbled by the sight of an important general who had been reduced to begging in the streets. Upon Francis's release he decided to devote himself to caring for lepers, the poor, and the sick. Seeking out the impoverished general who had inspired his new commitment, Francis exchanged his fine clothing for the begger general's cloak of rags. He was stoned in the streets by children who thought he was insane. One day, while Francis prayed in a run-down church, a voice issued from the crucifix and directed Francis to "rebuild my church." Francis took the words literally and renovated the building, using money from his family's fortune and infuriating his father, who thought he'd gone mad.

Francis hid in a cave to escape the wrath of his father, who had reached his limit with Francis's unconventional behavior and overexpenditures and went with a bishop to talk some sense into his son. Upon seeing his father, Francis ripped off his clothes, anxious to repay his father with the only property he possessed. The shocked bishop covered Francis with his own cape.

Francis was disinherited and began his new religious life living in a tiny cell, wearing little more than a brown, coarse cloak, held together by rope, and a pair of drawers. He attracted hordes of young followers who were drawn to his pleasant face, merry disposition, and relaxed lifestyle. Though Francis publicly proclaimed poverty as his wife, his symbolic marriage did not free him from temptations of the flesh. To defend himself, he took to rolling naked in the snow and hurling himself upon thorny rosebushes, which seeded wherever drops of his blood fell on the ground.

Francis was famous for founding the Franciscan order, in which members gave up everything they

owned and lived on gifts of food while they preached love and tolerance. Francis performed many miracles, the best known perhaps being his sermons to the birds, who indicated their understanding of his words by flying away in a cross formation. He tried on various occasions, in fact, to convert wild animals and did tame a wild wolf that was ravaging the town of Gubbio. His sensitivity to and love for all things was universal: He would not blow out a candle lest he hurt the flame.

After a forty-day fast, the marks of the stigmata appeared on his body and did not fade until his death. When his tomb was opened, Francis's body stood upright with its eyes wide open in contemplation. Francis is often portrayed receiving the marks of the stigmata, preaching to animals, or looking at a skull.

FOURTH CENTURY

SAINT PELAGIA

Feast day: October 8

A licentious dancing girl and actress of scandalous reputation, Pelagia drew the attention of the local bishop, who used the vixen's vanity and coquetry as a lesson in humility for his clergy. By chance, Pelagia heard a different sermon by the same bishop and was moved to repent her wicked ways. She was baptized and took to dressing as a man, living the rest of her life in solitude in a cave.

There are also two other saints with this name: a second was a virgin from Antioch who threw herself into the sea to escape being raped by a gang of soldiers that surrounded her house; a third was martyred because she refused to become the emperor's concubine.

FOURTEENTH CENTURY

SAINT BRIDGET

(ALSO CALLED BRIGIT, BIRGITTA)

Feast day: October 8. Patron of Sweden; founder

of the Brigittines

Attributes: The habit of the Brigittines, carrying a

pilgrim's staff and scrip, and often a candle

Born to a rich landowner in Sweden, Bridget began having visions and religious dreams when she was a small child. Despite this early religious bent, she was married, by arrangement, at fourteen to a wealthy man and bore him eight children. For many years she helped to run the lush estates of her husband and to raise her brood, until one day the queen, Blanche of Nemur, requested she take on the position of head lady-in-waiting. Bridget's visions returned once she started life at court, and she began to make small pilgrimages to local shrines, often accompanied by her husband. Her husband was not long for the world, however, and after his death, Bridget went into solitary penitence to figure out what she should do.

After two years, Bridget decided to found her own order. She moved to Vadstena in 1346 and established a community of monks and nuns who lived in separate enclosures but shared the same church. Bridget's austerity was legendary: she slept on a bare mattress on the floor with little covering, dropped hot wax on her palms, slept and ate very little, and prayed continually. Bridget went to Rome three years later to receive the pope's approval for her order and never returned. She lived the rest of her days in Italy, making pilgrimages and writing of her visions and prophecies, and had the Bible translated into Swedish. A healer, Bridget also worked with the sick and needy. She died at age seventy-one.

Often depicted in the robes of the Brigittines—black robe, white veil, and red or black band across the forehead—Bridget carries the staff of an abbess, or the pilgrim's staff and scrip, and a candle.

S · BRIGITTA   S · CATHARINA   S · ELISABETH   S · ELISAB

SVECA   HVNGAR   PORTVG

FOURTH CENTURY

SAINT THAÏS

Feast day: October 8

An Egyptian prostitute who was converted by Saint Paphnutius, Thaïs set fire to all her possessions and gave away her all jewels and ill-gotten earnings. She then went to live in a small cell where she lived off bread and water thrust through a hole in the door. There she spent three years until Saint Paphnutius had a vision in which her sins were forgiven.

THIRD CENTURY

SAINT DENYS

(ALSO CALLED DENIS, DENNIS, DIONIS, DIONYSIUS)

Feast day: October 9. One of the Fourteen Holy Helpers; patron of France, bishop of Paris; One of the Seven Champions of Christendom

Attribute: Episcopal robes, carrying his head in his hands

Denys, an Italian sent on a mission to Gaul, became bishop of Paris. Denys and two colleagues, Eleutherius and Rusticus, lived on an island in middle of the Seine, building a bastion of Christianity that became quite threatening to the local pagan leaders. All three men were captured and beheaded at Montmartre (martyr's hill) during the Valerian persecutions, and their headless bodies were thrown into the Seine. Remarkably, Denys managed to surface and carry his own head two miles to the place where the cathedral of St. Denys now stands—the burial site of French kings.

The cult of Saint Denys was fueled by the Benedictines in the Middle Ages, but it gained momentum in the ninth century because of a treatise written by a Parisian abbot, who hoped to bring more fame to the cathedral by claiming that Denys was also Dionysius of Athens, an early Christian converted by Saint Paul. Although there is nothing to link the two saints, the treatise managed to connect Saint Denys with the origins of Christianity, making Paris a cornerstone in the religion's foundation.

ELEVENTH CENTURY

SAINT EDWARD

Feast day: October 13. King of England

Edward the Confessor became king of England in 1042 and preserved the peace in his country for twenty-four years. He was married but never con-summated the relationship, preferring to indulge his passions for the hunt. His holiness was first recorded by his citizens, to whom he was readily accessible. King Edward was known to have visions: one time, he gave a beggar a precious ring that was returned to him by John the Evangelist, in disguise, with a message of impending death. Edward was a generous king: waking up one night to see a thief robbing his treasury, Edward shooed the man out, with the loot, before the guards came. In addition, he apparently had the ability to cure scrofula (otherwise known as "the king's evil") by his mere touch. Using money from his own pocket, King Edward restored and expanded Westminster Abbey, which thereafter became the coronation and burial site for future English kings. Edward's tomb and shrine still lie there, unmoved by the centuries. In addition to Saint George, Edward is often considered a patron of England and is invoked in times of military threat. He was canonized in 1161.

SAINT URSULA AND THE ELEVEN THOUSAND VIRGINS

FOURTH CENTURY

SAINT URSULA

AND THE ELEVEN THOUSAND VIRGINS

Feast day: October 21. Patroness of orphans, school girls,
teachers, and the Ursuline Sisters

Attributes: School girls

Ursula, the daughter of the Christian king of Brittany, caught the fancy of a pagan British prince. Committed to God but afraid to refuse the powerful prince, Ursula accepted engagement to him under what she thought to be impossible conditions: a three-year delay to her nuptials and twelve ships, one to house herself and ten noble companions and eleven others equipped with one thousand handmaidens each. Surprisingly, the British agreed and dispatched the ships and maidens. After a lengthy pilgrimage in France and Rome, the maidens reboarded their vessels and were blown down the Rhine, landing at Cologne. There they were greeted by Huns who were under strict orders to kill all Christians. Loathe to murder such a wealth of youth and beauty, the chief of the Huns offered to marry Ursula and spare her, at least, but she refused. She joined her companions, and the entire party was slain with arrows.

THIRD CENTURY

CRISPIN AND CRISPINIAN

Feast day: October 25. Patrons of cobblers, shoemakers,
and leather workers

Two Roman brothers, Crispin and Crispinian made shoes for their food rather than live off charity, and preached their Christian faith throughout France. Since they had no money, angels brought them leather to work with each night. Shakespeare's *Henry V* refers to them before the Battle of Agincourt, which was fought on their feast day.

FIRST CENTURY

SAINT JUDE

(ALSO KNOWN AS THADDEUS)

Feast day: October 28. One of the twelve apostles; patron of desperate cases (replacing Saint Rita)

Attribute: A club

Although Jude was one of the twelve apostles, his name was unfortunately so similar to that of the betrayer Judas Iscariot that he was rarely invoked for anything, until he became the patron saint of people in despair. He is linked with Saint Simon, with whom he preached in Persia. Together they drove two devils out of a pagan temple. Jude was beaten to death with a club, and so he is frequently depicted in art holding one. He is often called upon to help find lost objects.

DATES UNKNOWN

SAINT QUENTIN

Feast day: October 31

The fifth child of a Roman senator, Quentin gave up command of an army when he converted to Christianity. He worked in France, at Amiens, preaching. There, he was martyred in several ghastly fashions: Red-hot nails were driven through his head and shoulders; his body was impaled on an iron spit; he was beheaded; and his head was thrown in a river with a millstone wrapped around it—his body soon followed.

Fifty years later Quentin's intact corpse resurfaced and was brought to shore by a blind woman, who buried it and regained her sight. He is buried on the hill where the city of Saint Quentin is located. Years later, a priest went to this site to pray for a man condemned to hang for stealing a horse. On the destined day, the noose broke and the man was saved.

S·DOMINICVS S·FRANCISCVS S·FERDINANDVS S·LVDOVICVS S·PETRVS S·ANTONIVS
ASSISIAS   HISPANIÆ   REX   NOLASCVS PATAVINVS

NOVEMBER

ALL SAINTS

Feast Day: November 1

The celebration of all saints in heaven, All Saints' Day is known in England as All Hallows' Day, and the evening before as All Hallows' Eve, the origin of the American festival of Halloween. The day following All Saints' Day is called All Souls' Day when Christians pray for souls in purgatory. These two days are also informally recognized as the beginning of winter.

SIXTH CENTURY

SAINT LEONARD

Feast day: November 6. Patron of women in labor and prisoners of war

Destined to become one of the most popular saints in the Middle Ages in Western Europe, Leonard was born into the French nobility and was groomed to become a bishop. He refused, preferring instead to build a small cell in what is now called Saint-Leonard, near Limoges. There he lived as a hermit, completely alone.

One afternoon, Leonard's godfather, King Clovis I, was hunting in a nearby forest with his pregnant wife when suddenly she went into a difficult labor. Leonard was called, and the baby was born safely because of his prayers. King Clovis was so grateful that he gave Leonard as much land as he could ride a donkey around within one night. On this bequest, Leonard built the abbey of Noblac, where he eventually died and was buried.

FOURTH CENTURY

SAINT MARTIN OF TOURS

Feast day: November 11. Patron of tailors and drunkards
Attributes: A goose, a ball of fire, and a cloak split in half

Martin was a devout Christian born in Pannonia (now Hungary) who was forced to join the Roman army. During this service, which took him to France, he was honored by Constantine the Great. One particularly bitter winter in Amiens, while Martin was still in the army, he encountered a starving, shivering beggar; he cut his warm cloak and gave half to the beggar (hence his patronage of tailors). That night he dreamed that Christ appeared dressed as the beggar in the half-cloak. Inspired, Martin applied to leave the army, so he could devote his life to contemplation. Not only did his superiors refuse, his friends and colleagues taunted him for cowardice. Martin responded by offering to fight unarmed at the front of

the battle lines, fronting his beliefs with nothing but a cross to prove his courage. Luckily, he was not put to this test because a sudden peace was declared (said to be by divine intervention), and the soldiers were released from service. Martin went to live on an island near Genoa until he was called back to France to become the bishop of Tours. Martin literally tried to hide from the responsibility, but was given away by the cackling of a goose in the barn where he lay. At Tours he lived in a small cell outside the city walls and became known for his outstanding charity and humility, as well as several miracles.

During Mass one day, Martin again surrendered his robes to a beggar who stood in the congregation, and upon raising the chalice toward heaven, a ball of fire appeared above his head and a gold film enveloped his arms. On another occasion, he reportedly refused a goblet of wine at an emperor's banquet, giving it to a poor parish priest instead, and thus became a patron to drunkards and winos. When Martin

SAINT MARTIN

died, the angels were said to have sung as they carried him to heaven. Martin was the first saint who was neither martyr nor reputed martyr.

Martin's feast day occurs during a time when many servants were hired to help slaughter livestock and salt it for winter. His day also coincides with the annual migration of geese in some parts and is occasionally celebrated with a goose dinner. Indian summer is commonly known throughout various parts of Europe as Saint Martin's Summer.

FOURTH CENTURY

SAINT MENNAS

Feast day: November 11. Patron of camels, camel drivers, and caravans in the desert

Attribute: A pair of camels

A soldier in the Roman army, Mennas was killed in Egypt for being a Christian. His shrine was a ma-

jor pilgrimage destination in Egypt until the Arab invasion in the seventh century. Vials of oil taken from a lamp at his shrine were taken home by pilgrims. Mennas is popular in the Middle East and Asia, and he is often invoked in times of military threat.

TWELFTH CENTURY

SAINT HUGH

Feast day: November 17

Attribute: A swan

There are two Hughs of Lincoln. The first Hugh of Lincoln (c. 1140-1200) lived out his life as a Carthusian monk and bishop. A man of legendary holiness and wisdom, Henry II heard about Hugh and asked the humble man to become the prior of his ailing Carthusian monastery. Hugh hesitantly took the job and, in the course of his service, turned the prospects of the house around; returned money and lands from local peasants, originally impounded to build the monastery; subdued his capricious monarch; and understandably made great friends with the people in his community. Hugh was a champion of the underdog and would often stand up to kings and their armies in defense of a solitary peasant. He buried the dead, attended sick children, nursed the lepers, and protected the Jews during a race riot at the turn of the twelfth century.

In art, this Hugh is seen with his pet swan, who refused to eat after his master died. The saint is infrequently pictured with a chalice purveying an image or figure of the baby Jesus, who supposedly appeared to Hugh during a sermon.

The other Hugh of Lincoln was a little nine-year-old boy who was tortured, crowned with thorns, and crucified. When the earth would not accept his body, his murderer threw it down a well. The ensuing accusations that this was a ritual murder committed by Jews were typical of the anti-Semitism of the era. "Little Hugh's" legend is told by Chaucer in his "Prioress's Tale" in *The Canterbury Tales.*

THIRTEENTH CENTURY

SAINT ELIZABETH

Feast day: November 19

Attribute: A basket or apronful of roses and a loaf of bread

The daughter of King Andrew II of Hungary, Elizabeth was only a baby when the court poet wrote a ballad prophesying her marriage to the landgrave of Thuringia, Louis IV. Her father liked the idea and engaged the infant to be married. Luckily, Elizabeth enjoyed what turned out to be a seemingly loving and fruitful marriage. She was vibrant, passionate, and engaging, bearing her husband four children in rapid succession. Despite her noble rank, she was severe in her own lifestyle, often wearing coarse cloth instead

SAINT ELIZABETH

of fine dresses and never wearing her crown. Elizabeth was legendary for her extraordinary generosity, always giving away almost everything she had—often to the irritation and scorn of her husband and his family. She founded hospitals and orphanages, and spent much of her time caring for the sick and needy. Her personal habits did little to ingratiate her to her husband's family, who mocked and humiliated her and tried to prevent her from becoming queen.

Once, after a particularly frenzied period of almsgiving, Elizabeth found herself with nothing to wear to a court function but an old cloak. As she bravely walked toward the court hall, her cloak miraculously transformed into a royal cape. In a different instance, her mother-in-law attempted to entrap Elizabeth when the young girl was treating a leper in her bedroom; when her mother-in-law threw open the doors to Elizabeth's chamber, the leper had turned into a carved figure of the Crucifixion. During a viciously cold winter, Elizabeth risked her

health to take food and clothing to the poor. On one such visit, she was stopped by her enraged and worried husband, but the basket of food she was carrying turned into roses—thus her attribute.

Elizabeth's life took a dramatic turn for the worse when her husband died of the plague during a crusade. Her brother-in-law, accusing her of squandering the family fortune on ne'er-do-wells, promptly threw her out on the streets with her children, forcing the family to live in a pigsty the first few weeks of their exile. He directed every citizen not to take her in, and eventually she settled down to extreme poverty in a small cottage on the edge of town. Distraught and humiliated but still beautiful, Elizabeth turned her back on offers of marriage and chose instead to become a Franciscan, placing herself under the direction of a cruel and much-despised confessor, Conrad of Marburg. Conrad heartlessly sent Elizabeth's children away and dismissed her two favorite companions, substituting them with two ill-tempered women whose task it was to insult Elizabeth and beat her for any infractions. She lived out the short remainder of her life knitting, spinning, and working in hospitals, all the while under Conrad's strict orders of fasts and penance. Eventually Elizabeth's husband's colleagues returned from the crusade, charged with the duty of protecting her. As they prepared to reinstate her, her brother-in-law relented and recognized his nephew, Elizabeth's son. All this was too late for Elizabeth: she died from the self-imposed austerity of her life at the age of twenty-four.

In art, Elizabeth is shown carrying a bouquet of red roses in her skirt and a loaf of bread behind her, or holding a double crown. Frequently she is also illustrated amid a group of beggars. Her relics are preserved at Marburg, which was the center of her popular cult until the 1539.

THIRD CENTURY
SAINT CECILE
(ALSO CALLED CECILIA, CELIA, CECILY)

Feast day: November 22, known internationally as a day of music. Patroness of musicians and the Academy of Music in Rome
Attributes: An organ, a lute, a scroll of music, and a crown of lilies and roses

A famous virgin whose legend was retold by Chaucer as the "Second Nun's Tale" in *The Canterbury Tales*, Cecile was contracted to be married although she had secretly committed herself to celibacy. On the day of her wedding she was unable to stop the ceremony, but that night she refused to consummate her marriage. Her new husband agreed to respect her wishes if she could prove her faith. She asked him to visit her bishop (Pope) Urban, and

SAINT CECILE

SAINT CECILE

when he returned much impressed, she led him into the bridal chamber that had been transformed, amazingly, by heavenly music, fragrance, and flowers. An angel presented Cecile with a crown of roses and lilies; her husband was instantly converted.

In honor of this wildly popular saint, Dryden wrote "Song for Saint Cecile's Day" and Alexander Pope composed "Ode for Music on Saint Cecilia's Day."

FOURTH CENTURY

SAINT CATHERINE

Feast day: November 25. One of the Fourteen Holy Helpers; patroness of unmarried women, students, philosophers, nurses, and craftsmen who use a wheel (potters, spinners, millers)

Attribute: A wheel

The daughter of a pagan princess in Egypt, Catherine of Alexandria reportedly had a halo already encircling her head when she was born. As she grew, Catherine immersed herself in a meditative, studious life and became a quiet and quite beautiful girl. When she was fourteen her father died, making her the queen. This advancement in society led to numerous offers of marriage, which she repeatedly deferred. Around this time, it was rumored that the Virgin Mary had presented herself in a vision to a hermit and ordered him to find Catherine and tell her that she had been chosen to become a bride of Christ. The hermit gallantly made his way into the queen's quarters and, while showing her a picture of the Madonna and child, told the queen his message. Catherine was instantly converted.

A new but devoted believer, Catherine energetically protested the persecution of Christians by the emperor Maxentius. The emperor responded by lusting after Catherine with equal determination. Catherine continued to decline any physical

advances and enraged her suitor with her impenetrability. The emperor called in fifty philosophers to argue Catherine from her beliefs; she successfully debated them all. He then threw Catherine into prison to starve; she responded by converting not only her attendants but the empress as well. The emperor executed his wife for heresy and,

perversely, proposed marriage to Catherine. When she firmly, and finally, refused, he ordered the girl to be ripped apart between spiked wheels. As she was placed between the teeth of the wheels, a lightning bolt erupted from the sky, smiting the wheels and shattering them into a million pieces, injuring many bystanders. The emperor immediately ordered Catherine to be beheaded, and milk—not blood—was said to have flowed from her severed head.

One of the most popular saints of the Middle Ages, Catherine's grisly death and honorable life made her a great favorite of artists and writers, who have memorialized her image throughout the Christian world. Catherine is widely depicted in art with a wheel, the origin of the "catherine wheel" fireworks, and with a sword, books, scientific instruments, globes, and maps. The mystical marriage of Saint Catherine was also a popular subject in art from the fourteenth century: she is shown accepting a wedding ring from the Christ child, who leans toward her from Mary's lap. Catherine is invoked to protect the dying.

S. Andreas.

FIRST CENTURY

SAINT ANDREW

Feast day: November 30. One of the twelve apostles;
one of the Seven Champions of Christendom; patron
of Scotland, Greece, and Russia
Attributes: The saltire cross, a coil of rope, white hair,
and a long white beard

Andrew was a fisherman and disciple of John the Baptist before he began serving Jesus. It was Andrew who found the boy whose meager provision of fish enabled Jesus to feed five thousand in the miracle of the loaves and fishes. Andrew performed many miracles of his own, such as freeing the inhabitants of Nicea from seven demons who attacked them in the bodies of wild dogs. He survived being thrown to several different kinds of beasts in the ring. Andrew could strike people blind, but he also was said to have cured the sight

of Saint Matthew and to have saved a bishop from consorting with the devil, who had come to him in the form of a beautiful woman, by interrupting the two just as they sat down for a romantic dinner.

Saint Andrew met his end when he cured and then converted the wife of a pagan man who did not enjoy his wife's new chastity. Andrew was put in jail, beaten with seven scourges, and bound to a cross at Patras— a saltire cross, in the form of an X rather than a T.

Andrew's relics were taken to Constantinople, but some of his bones found their way to the city of Fife in Scotland. Fife is now the seaside town of Saint Andrew's, home to the university of the same name. Andrew became the patron saint of Scotland when the nation was victorious in a war against England, after a Saint Andrew's cross appeared in the sky. The white cross against a blue background is the emblem on the Scottish national flag and also represents Scotland on the Union Jack of Great Britain.

DECEMBER

SEVENTH CENTURY

SAINT ELOI

(ALSO CALLED ELIGIUS)

Feast day: December 1. Patron of metalworkers

Attributes: A horseshoe, or holding the devil by the nose
with a pair of tweezers

A skilled and pious goldsmith from Limoges, France, Saint Eloi designed and decorated the thrones, tombs, and shrines of kings and the clergy. He once made two thrones out of the gold allocated for one. Because of his thrifty skill and trustworthiness, he was made master of the royal mint. His generosity was paramount: it was said that one could tell where Saint Eloi's house by the line of beggars streaming through the gate. In due time, Eloi slowly turned away from his art in favor of more spiritual pursuits. He became a bishop, founding monasteries in Paris, Noyen, and Solignac. He was steadfast in his preachings against such pagan activities as palm reading and fortune telling, as well as in enforcing Sunday as a day of rest. A dangerous horse possessed by the devil was once brought to him to be shod. Instead of risking being kicked, Eloi skillfully sliced off the horse's leg and put the shoe on its foot at his leisure. When he finished, he calmly reattached the leg to its owner. He is represented in art with a horseshoe, often enacting this famous miracle. Artists also show him leading the devil around by the nose with a pair of pincers.

S. Éloi compagnon orfèvre excelle dans
l'art de travailler les Métaux.

FOURTH CENTURY

SAINT BARBARA

Feast day: December 4. Patroness of architects,
gunsmiths, firefighters, and artillery men
Attributes: A sword, a cannon, a host, a chalice,
and a peacock feather

Barbara was a stunning beauty whose possessive father locked her up in a steep tower, away from the eager eyes of any suitors. Shuttered away, Barbara turned to contemplation and became a Christian. During one of her father's absences, she had workmen put in a third window in her tower as a sign of the Holy Trinity. Her father returned and read the symbolism on the wall. To escape his rage, Barbara fled to the upper-

most part of the tower and was carried by angels to a hiding place. A shepherd gave her away, and his flock turned into grasshoppers. Rather than kill her himself, Barbara's father handed the maiden over to the government to be tortured. She was scourged with whips that transmuted into peacock feathers before they touched her flesh; she did not recant her new faith. Infuriated, Barbara's father marched her to the top of a mountain and smote off her head. He was struck dead by a thunderbolt simultaneously. For this reason, Barbara is invoked during thunderstorms and explosions, and, fittingly, became the patron of gunmen. The host and chalice symbolize Barbara's power to protect those in danger of dying before they receive the final blessings of Extreme Unction.

FOURTH CENTURY

SAINT NICHOLAS

Feast day: December 6. Patron of children,

pawnbrokers, perfumiers, sailors, and Russia

Attributes: Three golden balls, an anchor

Saint Nicholas is one of the most widely venerated saints in the world due to his association with Father Christmas. Although there is no evidence that Saint Nicholas rewarded children by bringing them toys in the middle of the night, he is responsible for many equally astonishing miracles. A bishop in Asia Minor, Nicholas was born to aristocrats and died at Myra. His parents knew from the moment he was born that he would lead a religious life when he stood on his infant legs to praise God and refused to nurse on fast days. When he inherited his family's money, Nicholas distributed it to the poor. Nicholas heard the plight of a

recently impoverished neighbor, who was afraid his three daughters would have to become prostitutes through lack of funds, and went to the house on three successive nights to toss a bag of gold through the window so that the daughters might marry. The pawnbroker's symbol of three balls is taken from this legend and, thus, Nicholas has become their patron saint.

A patron to little children and sailors, as well, Nicholas once resurrected three boys who had been kidnapped by an innkeeper during a famine and then killed and salted to be used as food for the innkeeper's guests. Nicholas, himself staying the night at this inn, knew what the food was without touching it. He went to the basement and raised the boys out of the brine tub.

Nicholas answered the prayers of the crew on a sinking ship by leading it safely to land. His association with the sea began when he undertook an ocean voyage and, disturbed by the activity of the waves, commanded them to be still—which they did. His popularity with seafarers is evident by the number of harbor churches dedicated to him. In Bari, Italy, the final resting place of some of the saint's relics, the feast of Saint Nicholas is kept by sailing an image of the saint out to sea and bringing it back at night accompanied by a torchlit procession. His relics are said to give off a myrrh-like scent with healing properties, and so he is also the patron of perfumiers. Nicholas can be invoked for protection against robbery.

The legend of "Saint Nick," or Santa Claus, is primarily the invention of Dutch Protestants, but became tremendously popular in Britain and America during the Victorian era. In Germany, Sweden, and the Netherlands, children who leave empty shoes and stockings out on the feast day of Saint Nicholas awake to find them filled with gifts and treats. Despite the many different stories, there is no doubt that Saint Nicholas, in his generous, expansive, and selfless nature, epitomizes the essential spirit of Christmas.

FOURTH CENTURY
SAINT LUCY

(ALSO CALLED LUCIA)

Feast day: December 13

Attributes: Eyes, a lamp, or a lantern

Lucy was a wealthy Sicilian woman who ardently refused many marriage offers and was reported to the town governor by one of her rejected suitors. The governor ordered her into a brothel to be violated, but her body remained miraculously locked; she did not move even when pulled by a team of oxen. In some versions of her life, her eyes were torn out and restored by angels. In others, Lucy plucked them out herself to protect her body from further shame, and sent the orbs to the suitor who betrayed her. In either case, Lucy was unsuccessfully burnt at the stake and, finally, executed with a sword.

Her name is derived from "lux" or "light," and so Lucy has become associated with festivals and

celebrations of light. Before the Gregorian reform of the calendar, her feast day occurred on the shortest day of the year. Then and now (especially in Sweden), her feast day is celebrated by the youngest daughter donning a crown of burning candles and waking the rest of the family with coffee, special rolls, and a little song. Lucy is invoked to help those afflicted with eye disease.

EIGHTH CENTURY
SAINT IRMINA

Feast day: December 24

Princess Irmina, daughter of Saint Dagobert II, was engaged to marry a handsome young count. On the eve of her wedding, one of her officers, who was secretly—and madly—in love with her, convinced her fiancé to accompany him up a steep cliff outside the town. There, the officer declared his passion and tried to fling the count over the embankment. In the fierce struggle that ensued, both men were swept off the cliff. After this tragic denouement to a marriage she had eagerly anticipated, Irmina asked permission to become a nun. Her father restored a building and established a convent for her near Trier, Germany.

FOURTH CENTURY

SAINT ANASTASIA

(ALSO CALLED PHARMACOLYTRIA)

Feast day: December 25

A Roman matron of noble birth to whom many adventures are attributed, Anastasia was eventually arrested for helping Christian prisoners and, as punishment, sent out to sea in a leaky boat with a throng of slaves. Intervention by Saint Theodora led the boat safely to land. All of the slaves, having been converted by Anastasia's bravery and faith during their ordeal, were beheaded by their owners upon landing. Anastasia was taken to an island (perhaps within present-day Croatia), where she was bound to a saltire cross, her breasts were cut off, and she was burned to death. Invocation of her name supposedly renders poison innocuous.

THIRD CENTURY

SAINT EUGENIA

Feast day: December 25

Daughter of the Duke of Alexandria, Eugenia was a great scholar who wished to continue learning under the tutelage of monks. She dressed herself as a man in order to become a monk and achieved such success that she was later made an abbot. Accused of philandering, she was brought to trial before her father but proved her innocence (and lost her job) by disrobing, revealing her true gender and identity. She was eventually beheaded in Rome under Emperor Severus.

St. Stephen

FIRST CENTURY

SAINT STEPHEN

Feast day: December 26. One of the seven deacons;
the first Christian martyr
Attributes: Often pictured beside Saint Laurence
with the books of the Gospel, stones, and the palm
of martyrdom

Stephen was one of the men whom the apostles appointed to govern the first Christian community, collect alms, and aid the poor, while the apostles spent their days in prayer and ministry of the Gospel. He spoke with such eloquence and passion that he quickly gathered a large following, criticizing the Temple of Jerusalem by declaring that "God cannot be contained by human-built walls." Stephen was put on trial by the Jewish council of elders for blasphemy. After he gave a lengthy speech in which he castigated his jurors for killing Jesus, the council cast him out of the city and stoned him. At his death he requested that the sins of his murderers be not charged against them, a prayer that eventually played a large part in the conversion of Saint Paul, who stood among his persecutors.

Stephen's body was rescued right after his death and buried in an unmarked grave. Centuries later a priest was told he would find the grave of Saint Stephen by the clusters of red roses that bloomed year-long beside it. Once found, Stephen's body was taken to the basilica of the church of San Lorenzo in Rome and interred in the same tomb as Saint Laurence.

Stephen is the patron of deacons and is invoked against headaches, perhaps because his name means "crown" in Greek. The cycle of his life was painted by Fra Angelico at the Vatican.

A List of Patron Saints

Accountants: Matthew
Actors: Genesius·
Advertisers: Bernardine of Siena
Agricultural workers: Phocas, Walstan
Airmen and air passengers: Our Lady of Loreto, Joseph
   of Cupertino
Air travelers: Joseph of Cupertino
Altar boys: John Berchmans
Anesthetists: Rene Goupil
Animals and birds: Francis of Assisi
Animals (sick): Beuno
Apothecaries: Nicholas
Archaeologists: Damasus, Jerome
Archers: George, Sebastian
Architects: Thomas the Apostle, Barbara
Art: Catherine of Bologna
Artists: Luke
Astronauts: Joseph of Cupertino
Astronomers: Dominic
Athletes: Sebastian
Authors: Francis de Sales
Bakers: Elizabeth of Hungary
Bankers: Matthew
Barbers: Cosmas and Damian
Barren women: Antony of Padua
Basket makers: Antony the Abbot
Beekeepers: Ambrose, Bernard, Modomnoc

Beggars: Alexis, Martin of Tours, Benedict Labre, Giles
Bishops: Ambrose, Charles Borromeo
Blacksmiths: Dunstan, Eloi, Giles, Brigid
Blind: Lucy, Dunstan, Raphael
Boatmen: Julian the Hospitaller
Bookbinders: Peter Celestine
Bookkeepers: Matthew
Booksellers: John of God, Thomas Aquinas
Boy scouts: George
Boys: Nicholas, Aloysius
Bricklayers: Stephen
Brides: Nicholas of Myra
Broadcasters: Archangel Gabriel
Brush makers: Antony
Builders: Vincent Ferrer
Bursars: Joseph
Cab drivers: Fiacre
Cabinetmakers: Anne
Cancer victims: Peregrine Laziosi
Canonists: Raymond of Penafort
Carpenters: Joseph
Charitable societies: Elizabeth of Hungary,
   Vincent de Paul
Childbirth: Gerard Majella, Margaret of
   Antioch
Children: Nicholas, Lambert, Genevieve
Choirboys: Dominic Savio
Church: Joseph, Peter
Clerics: Gabriel
Cloth workers: Homobonus
Coachmen: Richard of Chichester
Cobblers: Crispin and Crispinian

SAINT MATTHIAS

SAINT MATTHEW

Comedians: Vitus

Confessors: Alphonsus Liguori, John Nepomucene

Convulsive children: Scholastica

Cooks: Laurence, Martha

Cripples: Giles, Gilben of Sempringham

Dancers: Vitus

Dairymaids: Brigid

Deacons: Laurence, Stephen

Deaf: Francis de Sales

Dentists: Apollonia

Desperate cases: Jude, Rita of Cascia

Dietitians: Martha

Diplomats: Gabriel

Doctors: Luke, Cosmas and Damian

Dogs (healthy): Huben

Dogs (mad): Sithnq

Domestic animals: Antony

Druggists: Cosmas and Damian

Dyers: Maurice and Lydia

Dying: Barbara, Joseph, Margaret

Dysentery sufferers: Matrona

Earthquakes: Emygdius

Ecologists: Francis of Assisi

Ecumenists: Cyril and Methodius, Josan

Editors: John Bosco

Emigrants: Frances Xavier Cabrini

Engineers: Ferdinand III

Epileptics: Dympna, Vitus

Expectant mothers: Gerard Majella

Eye trouble: Lucy, Cyriacus

Falsely accused: Raymund Nonnatus

Farmers: Isidore the Farmer

Farriers: John the Baptist, Eloi

Fathers: Joseph

Firefighters: Agatha, Laurence, Flonan, Barbara

Fire prevention: Catherine of Siena

First communicants: Tarcisius

Fishermen: Andrew, Peter, Simon, Nicholas

Florists: Dorothy, Rose of Lima, Therese of
    Lisieux

Foresters: John Gualbert

Founders: Barbara

Foundlings: Holy Innocents

Fullers: Anastasius the Fuller

Funeral directors: Joseph of Arimathea

Gardeners: Adelard, Fiacre, Phocas

Girls: Agnes, Catherine, Nicholas, Ursula

Glassworkers: Luke

Goldsmiths: Dunstan, Eloi

Gravediggers: Antony the Abbot

Grocers: Michael

Gunners: Barbara

Hairdressers: Martin de Porres

Headache sufferers: Teresa of Avila, Gereon, Stephen,
    Acacius

Heart patients: John of God

Hermits: Antony, Giles, Hilarion

Holy death: Joseph

Homeless: Benedict, Joseph Labre

Horses: Giles, Hippolytus

Hospitals: Camillus de Lellis, John of God, Armel

Hotel keepers: Amand, Julian, Manha

Housekeepers: Anne, Martha, Zita

Hunters: Hubert, Eustace

Husbands: George

Infantry: Maurice

Intestinal disease sufferers: Erasmus
Invalids: Roch
Jewelers: Eligius, Eloi
Journalists: Francis de Sales
Jurists: John of Capistrano
Kings: Edward, Louis, Henry
Knights: George, James the Great
Laborers: Isidore
Lawyers: Hilary, Thomas More, Yves
Learning: Ambrose
Leather workers: Crispin and Crispinian
Lepers: Giles
Librarians: Jerome
Lighthouse keepers: Clement, Dunstan, Venerius
Locksmiths: Dunstan
Lost articles: Antony of Padua
Lovers: Valentine
Maidens: Catherine
Mariners: Nicholas
Married women: Monica
Medical technicians: Albert the Great
Mentally ill: Dympna
Merchants: Nicholas, Homobonus
Messengers: Gabriel
Midwives: Raymund Nonnatus, Pantaleon, Brigid
Millers: Arnulph
Miners: Barbara
Missions: Francis Xavier, Therese of Lisieux, Leonard
    of Port Maurice (parish)
Mothers: Blessed Virgin Mary, Giles, Monica
Motorists: Christopher
Mountaineers: Bernard of Menthon
Musicians: Cecilia, Gregory the Great

Mystics and mystical theologians: John of the Cross
Notaries: Luke, Mark
Nuns: Blessed Virgin Mary, Scholastica
Nurses: Agatha, Camillus, Elizabeth of Hungary, John
    of God, Catherine
Orators: John Chrysostom
Orphans: Jerome Emiliani, Ursula
Painters: Luke
Paralytics: Osmund
Paratroopers: Michael
Parish priests: John Vianney
Pawnbrokers: Nicholas
Penitents: Mary Magdalene
Perfumiers: Nicholas
Pharmacists: Cosmas and Damian
Philosophers: Catherine, Justin
Physicians: Cosmas and Damian, Luke
Pilgrims: James, Mennas
Plasterers: Bartholomew
Poets: Brigid, David, Columba, John of the Cross
Police: Michael
Poor: Antony of Padua, Laurence, Martin Porres
Popes: Peter, Gregory the Great
Porters: Christopher
Postal workers: Gabriel
Preachers: Catherine of Alexandria, John Chrysostom
Pregnant women: Margaret of Antioch
Priests: John Vianney
Printers: Augustine, Genesius, John of God
Prisoners: Dismas, Roch
Prisoners of war: Leonard
Prisons: Joseph Cafasso
Public relations: Bernardine of Siena

Publishers: John the Evangelist
Radiologists: Michael
Radio workers: Gabriel
Retreats: Ignatius
Rheumatism sufferers: James the Greater
Saddlers: Crispin and Crispinian
Sailors: Brendan, Erasmus, Nicholas, Francis of Paola, Phocas
Scholars: Brigid, Jerome
Scientists: Albert the Great
Sculptors: Claude
Secretaries: Mark, Genesius
Seminarians: Charles Borromeo
Servants: Martha, Zita
Shepherds: Cuthbert, Bernadene
Shoemakers: Crispin and Crispinian
Sick: John of God, Camillus de Lellis
Silversmiths: Andronicus, Dunstan
Singers: Cecilia, Gregory
Skaters: Lidwina
Skiers: Bernard of Menthon
Skin diseases: Marculf
Social justice: Joseph
Social workers: Louise de Marillac
Soldiers: George, Martin of Tours, Sebastian
Starving: Antony of Padua
Stonecutters: Clement
Stonemasons: Barbara, Four Crowned Martyrs, Reinhold, Stephen
Students: Catherine, Thomas Aquinas
Surgeons: Cosmas and Damian, Luke
Swordsmiths: Maurice

Syphilis sufferers: Fiacre, George
Tailors: Homobonus, Martin of Tours
Tanners: Crispin and Crispinian, Simon
Tax collectors: Matthew
Teachers: Gregory the Great, John Baptist de La Salle, Ursula
Telecommunications workers: Gabriel
Television: Clare
Television workers: Gabriel
Theologians: Augustine, John the Evangelist, Thomas Aquinas, Alphonsus
Throat sufferers: Blaise
Tinworkers: Joseph of Arimathea
Toothache sufferers: Apollonia, Medard, Osmund
Tramps: Benedict, Joseph Labre
Travelers: Christopher, Julian

SAINT PAUL

Vocations: Alphonsus
Virgins: Blessed Virgin Mary
Watchmen: Peter of Alcantara
Weavers: Maurice, Bernardino of Siena
Widows: Monica, Paula
Winegrowers: Morand, Vincent
Wine merchants: Amand, Vincent
Women in labor: Anne, Leonard
Women, unhappily married: Wilgefortis, Rita of Cascia
Working men: Joseph
Writers: John the Evangelist, Francis de Sales
Yachtsmen: Adjutor
Youth: Aloysius Gonzaga, John Bosco

MAJOR SAINTS AND THEIR FEAST DAYS

The following is a listing of major saints and their feast days; it is by no means exhaustive and a majority of those listed do not appear in this volume.

JANUARY

1: Almachius, Odilo
2: Basil, Gregory of Nazianzus, Munchin, Seraphim of Sarov
3: Genevieve
4: Elizabeth Seton
5: John Neumann, Amelie, Simeon
6: Peter of Canterbury
7: Lucian, Raymund of Pennafort
8: Abo, Pega, Severinus
9: Fillan
10: Paul the Hermit
11: Theodosius
12: Benedict Biscop, Salvius
13: Hilary
14: Felix of Nola, Macrina the Elder
15: Ita
16: Fursey, Marcellus, Sigebert
17: Antony of Egypt, Sulpicius
18: Prisca, Ulfrid, Margaret of Hungary
19: Henry of Finland, Wulfstan
20: Fabian, Sebastian, Euthymius the Great
21: Agnes
22: Vincent of Saragossa, Anastasius
23: Emerentiana, John the Almsgiver
24: Babylas, Francis of Sales
25: Paul, Praejectus, Juventinus and Maximinus
26: Conan, Paula, Timothy and Titus
27: Angela, Julian of Le Mans, Anthony
28: John the Sage, Thomas Aquinas
29: Gildas
30: Bathilde, Martina
31: John Bosco, Maedoc of Ferns

FEBRUARY

1: Brigid
2: Joan de Lestonnac
3: Anskar, Blaise, Ia, Laurence of Canterbury, Margaret of England
4: Gilbert of Sempringham, Phileas
5: Agatha
6: Amand, Dorothy, Mel, Paul Miki, Vedast
7: Richard, Romuald
8: Cuthman, Jerome Emiliani, Kew
9: Apollonia, Teilo
10: Scholastica
11: Gregory II, Benedict of Aniane
12: Julian the Hospitaller
13: Catherine dei Ricci
14: Conran, Cyril and Methodius, Valentine
15: Sigfrid
16: Juliana, Benedict, Joseph Labre
17: Finan of Lindisfarne, Fintan of Clonenagh, Loman, The Seven Servite Founders
18: Colman of Lindisfarne, Flavian
19: Boniface
20: Wulfric
21: Peter Damian

22: Margaret of Cortona
23: Milburga, Polycarp
24: Matthias, Montanus and Lucius, Prix
25: Ethelbert of Kent, Walburga
26: Alexander of Alexandria
27: Leander
28: Oswald of Worcester

MARCH

1: David
2: Chad
3: Winwaloe, Cunegund, Marinus
4: Adrian of May, Casimir, Owin
5: Ciaran of Saighir Piran
6: Colette, Chrodegang, Cyneburg, Conon, Perpetua and Felicity
8: Felix of Dunwich, John of God, Senan

9: Constantine, Forty Martyrs of Sebastea, Frances of Rome, Gregory of Nyssa, Dominic Savio
10: John Ogilvie
11: Oengus
12: Gregory, Paul Aurelian, Maximilian, Pionius
13: Gerald
14: Matilda, Leobinus
15: Longinus, Louise de Marillac, Zacharias
16: Abraham Kidunaia, Julian of Antioch
17: Patrick
18: Christian, Cyril, Edward the Martyr
19: Alemund, Joseph
20: Cuthbert, Herbert
21: Benedict, Enda, Nicholas of Flue
22: Zachary, Nicholas Owen
23: Turibius of Lima
24: Catherine of Vadstana
25: Alfwold, Dismas
26: Ludger, William of Norwich
27: John of Egypt
28: Tutilo, Thomas Acquinas
29: Gladys, Rupert, Ludolf
30: Amadée, Osburga, Zosimus of Syracuse
31: Benjamin, Acacius

APRIL

1: Hugh of Grenoble, Gilbert of Caithness
2: Francis of Paola, Mary of Egypt
3: Pancras of Taormina, Richard of Chichester, Agape, Irene and Chione
4: Ambrose, Isidore
5: Vincent Ferrer
6: William of Eskhill, Celestine I,

7: John Baptist de La Salle
8: Dionysius of Corinth, Julia
9: Waudru
10: Macarius, Fulbert
11: Guthlac, Stanislas, Gemma
12: Zeno of Verona
13: Martin I, Carpus and Papylus
14: Caradoc, Tiburtius and Companions
15: Hunna
16: Bernadette, Magnus
17: Donnan, Robert of the Chaise Diue, Stephen
    Harding
18: Apollonius, Laserian
19: Alphege, Leo IX
20: Agnes
21: Anselm
22: Theodore of Sykeon, Opportuna
23: George
24: Egbert, Fidelis, Ives

25: Mark
26: Cletus and Marcellinus
27: Zita
28: Peter Chanel
29: Endellion, Hugh of Cluny, Peter the Martyr, Robert
    of Molesme, Wilfrid II
30: Catherine of Siena

MAY

1: Corentin, Joseph the Workman
2: Athanasius
3: Philip, James the Lesser
4: Monica, Pelagia of Tarsus, Florian
5: Hilary
6: Edbert, Marian, John
7: Stanislaus
8: Acacius, Peter of Tarentaise
9: Gregory Nazianzen
10: Catald and Conleth, Antoninus
12: Nereus and Achilleus
13: Robert Bellarmine
14: Boniface of Tarsus, Pontius, Carthage
15: Dympha
16: Brendan the Navigator, Carantoc, Peregrine of
    Auxerre, Simon Stock
17: Madron, Paschal, Bruno
18: Eric of Sweden, Felix
19: Dunstan, Peter Celestine, Pudentiana, Yves
20: Bernardino of Siena, Ethelbert of East Anglia
21: Godric, Andrew Bobola
22: Humility, Rita
23: William
24: David of Scotland

25: Madeleine Barat, Gregory VII, Zenobius
26: Augustine of Canterbury, Philip Neri, Prix
27: Bede, Julius the Veteran
28: Augustine of Canterbury, Bernard of Montjoux
29: Mary Magdelen Dei Pazzi
30: Hubert, Joan of Arc, Ferdinand, Isaac
31: Queenship of the Virgin Mary, Petronilla

JUNE

1: Justin, Nicomedes, Wistan
2: Erasmus, Marcellinus and Peter
3: Kevin, Charles Lwanga and Companions
4: Petroc
5: Boniface
6: Norbert
7: Meriadok, Robert
8: Medard, William of York
9: Columba, Primus and Felician, Pelagia of Antioch
10: Margaret of Scotland, Ithamar
11: Barnabas
12: Eskil, Odulf
13: Antony of Padua
14: Basil, Dogmael
15: Trillo, Vitus, Modestus and Companions, Edburga, Germaine
16: Cyricus
17: Adulf, Emily, Harvey
18: Mark and Marcellian
19: Gervase and Protase, Juliana Falconieri
20: Edward the Martyr
21: Alban
22: Ralph, Thomas More
23: Agrippina, Audrey

24: Bartholomew of Farne, John the Baptist (nativity)
25: Adalbert
26: John and Paul, Salvius
27: Cyril of Alexandria, Samson, Zoilus
28: Irenaeus, Potamiaena
29: Elwin, Judith and Salome, Emma, Peter and Paul
30: Martyrs of Rome, Theobald of Provins

JULY

1: Julius and Aaron, Oliver Plunket, Serf
2: Visitation of the Virgin Mary, Processus and Maninian, Otto
3: Leo II, Julius and Aaron
4: Bertha, Odo
5: Antony Zaccaria
6: Dominica, Newlyn, Sexburga
7: Thomas of Canterbury
8: Grimbald, Elizabeth of Portugal
9: Adrian
10: Seven Holy Brothers
11: Benedict, Drostan, Olga
12: Nabor and Felix, Jason, Veronica
13: Mildred, Silas
14: Boniface of Savoy
15: Bonaventure, Vladimir, Henry
16: Helier
17: Alexis
18: Arnulf, Frederick
19: Vincent de Paul
20: Margaret of Antioch, Wilgefortis
21: Laurence of Brindisi, Victor
22: Mary Magdalene, Wandrille
23: Apollinaris, Bridget of Sweden

24: Christina, Boris and Gleb
25: Christopher, James the Greater
26: Joachim and Anne
27: Pantaleon, Seven Sleepers of Ephesus
28: Botvid, Samson
29: Lupus, Martha, Olaf, Faustus and Beatrice
30: Abdon and Sennen
31: Germanus of Auxerre, Ignatius, Neot

AUGUST

1: Alphonsus, Faith, Hope, and Charity, Maccabees
2: Etheldritha, Eusebius, Plegmund, Sidwell, Stephen I, Thomas of Hales
3: Manaccus, Waldef
4: Molua, Sithney, John Baptist Vianney
5: Afra
6: Sixtus
7: Cajetan
8: Dominic, Lide
9: Romanus (I)
10: Laurence
11: Alexander, Blane, Tiburtius and Susanna
12: Clare
13: Hippolytus
14: Fachanan, Maximilian Kolbe
15: The Assumption of the Virgin Mary, Arnulf, Tarsicius
16: Armel, Stephen of Hungary
17: Hyacinth, Roch
18: Agapitus, Helena
19: John Eudes, Mochta
20: Bernard, Oswin, Philbert

21: Pius X, Abraham of Smolensk
22: Sigfrid
23: Philip Benizi, Timothy and Companions
24: Bartholomew, Ouen
25: Mennas, Patrician, Genesius of Arles, Louis of France
26: Elizabeth Bichier des Ages, Zephyrinus
27: Monica, Caesarius of Arles
28: Augustine of Hippo, Hermes, Julian of Brioude
29: John the Baptist, Sebbi
30: Rose of Lima
31: Aidan of Lidistarne, Cuthburga

SEPTEMBER

1: Giles, Fiacre
2: Brocard
3: Gregory the Great
4: Marius, Ultan
5: Bertinus
6: Bega, Cagnoald, Laetus
7: Regina, Anastasius the Fuller, Cloud
8: Birthday of the Blessed Virgin Mary, Adrian and Natalia
9: Peter Claver, Gorgonius, Omer
10: Finnian of Moville, Nicholas of Tolentino
11: Paphnutius
12: Ailbe, Guy
13: John Chrysostom
14: Cornelius and Cyprian, Holy Cross
15: Catherine of Genoa
16: Cornelius, Cyprian, Edith
17: Hildegard, Lambert, Robert Bellarmine, Socrates and Stephen
18: Joseph of Cupertino
19: Januarius, Theodore of Canterbury
20: Eustace
21: Matthew
22: Laudus, Maurice, Thomas of Villanova
23: Thecla
24: Gerard
25: Cadoc, Finbar
26: Cyprian and Justina
27: Barry, Vincent de Paul, Cosmas and Damian
28: Lioba, Machan, Wenceslaus
29: Michael and All Angels
30: Honorius, Jerome

OCTOBER

1: Bavo, Mylor, Remi
2: Guardian Angels, Leger, Thomas of Hereford
3: Thérèsa
4: Francis of Assisi
5: Maurus and Placid
6: Bruno, Faith
7: Helen of Cornwall, Osith
8: Pelagia, Bridget, Thaïs
9: Denys, John Leonardi
10: Francis Borgia, Geron, Paulinus of York
11: Bruno
12: Edwin, Serafino, Wilfrid
13: Edward the Confessor, Gerald of Aurillac
14: Callistus, Justus
15: Albert, Thecla, Teresa of Avila
16: Gall, Hedwig, Lul, Gerard Majella
17: Margaret-Mary Alacoque, Ethelred and Ethelbricht, Etheldreda, Ignatius of Antioch, Nothelm, Rule
18: Gwen of Cornwall, John of Bridlington, Odoq Cluny
19: Cleopatra, Ethbin, Frideswide, Paul of the Cross, Peter of Alcantara, Ptolomaeus and Lucius
20 Edmund, Felix of Valois
21: Ursula, Hilarion
22: Donatus, Mellon
23: John of Capistrano, Severinus
24: Antony Claret, Felix of Thibiuca
25: Crispin and Crispinian, Forty Martyrs of England and Wales
26: Lucian and Marcian
27: Odhran

28: Simon and Jude, Salvius
29: Colman
30: Alphonsus and Rodríguez, Marcellus the Centurion
31: Foillan, Quentin, Wolfgang

NOVEMBER

1: All Saints, Benignus, Cadfan, Dingad, Gwymian, Vigor
2: All Souls
3: Clydog, Malachy, Pirmin, Manin de Porres, Rumwold, Winefride, Wulgan
4: Birstan, Charles Borromeo, Clether
5: Kea, Zachary and Elizabeth
6: Leonard, Melanie, Mennas, Winnoc
7: Engelbert, Willibrord
8: Four Crowned Martyrs, Godfrey
9: Theodore
10: Justus, Leo
11: Martin of Tours, Mennas
12: Josaphat, Lebuin
13: Abbo, Brice, Stanislaus Kostka, Homobonus, Nicholas I
14: Laurence O'Toole
15: Albert the Great, Fintan of Rheinau, Leopold of Austria
16: Edmund of Abingdon, Gertrude, Margaret of Scotland
17: Gregory of Tours, Gregory the Wonderworker, Hilda, Hugh of Lincoln, Zaccheus
18: Mabyn, Mawes, Odo
19: Elizabeth
20: Colman of Dromore, Edmund

21: Condedus
22: Cecile, Philemon and Apphia
23: Clement, Columbanus
24: Chrysogonus, Colman of Cloyne, Minver
25: Catherine
26: Silvester
27: Congar (I), Fergus, Virgil
28: Juthwara, Gregory III
29: Brendan of Birr
30: Andrew

"INSTRUMENTS DE SUPPLICE"

DECEMBER

1 : Eloi, Natalia
2 : Viviana
3 : Francis Xavier, Cassian
4 : Barbara, John Damascus, Osmund
5 : Christian of Markyate, Justinian, Crispina
6 : Nicholas
7 : Ambrose, Diuma
8 : Budoc
9 : Wolfeius
10 : Eulalia
11 : Damasus, Daniel the Stylite
12 : Finnian of Clonard, Jane Chantal
13 : Edburga of Minster, Judoc, Lucy
14 : Fingar, Hybald, John of the Cross, Nicasius, Venantius, Fortunatus
15 : Offa of Essex
16 : Bean (I)
17 : Lazarus
18 : Samthanth, Winnibald
21 : Peter Canisius, Thomas the Aposde, Beornwald
22 : Frances Cabrini
23 : Frithebert
24 : Irmina
25 : Alburga, Anastasia
26 : Stephen, Tathai
27 : John the Evangelist
28 : Holy Innocents
29 : Thomas of Canterbury
30 : Egwin
31 : Sylvester

GLOSSARY

ABBOT/ABBESS: The appointed leader of an abbey, the spiritual father or mother.

ABBEY: A monastery housing no fewer than twelve monks or nuns.

BEATIFICATION: The permission granted by the pope for a deceased person of extraordinary religious heroism to be venerated publicly. The step preceeding canonization.

BENEDICTINES: Monks (and nuns) of the Order of Saint Benedict established in Monte Cassino, Italy, in the sixth century. Great patrons of the arts and education, the order was known popularly as the "Black Monks." They follow the Rule of Saint Benedict and his sister, Saint Scholastica.

CANON: Rules and laws organizing life and discipline in the Church.

CANONIZATION: The inscription of the person's name in the catalogue of saints by the pope after a formal process of beatification and papal investigation. Canonization means a person is to be venerated in the liturgy.

CANTERBURY TALES: A collection of stories written in heroic couplets by Geoffrey Chaucer, begun in 1387 and unfinished at the author's death. Using many different narrators, the tales vividly tell of medieval life as seen through the eyes of a group of pilgrims on their way to the shrine of St. Thomas at Canterbury.

CATHOLIC: In the past referred to the entire body of Christians in the world, but today alludes to Roman Catholics: a group of Christians who believe that the pope in Rome is the Vicar of Christ.

CHALICE: The cup or vessel in which the wine of the Eucharist is consecrated.

CHRISTIAN: Followers of Christ, whom they believe is the Messiah.

CISTERCIAN ORDER: A branch of the Benedictine order established in Citeaux, France, by Robert Molêsmes. Also called the "White Monks."

COMMUNION: One of the sacraments, dedicated to celebrating the Last Supper, where a Christian receives a consecrated wafer (or Host) symbolizing, or embodying, the body of Christ; in some churches, the faithful also receive wine, symbolizing, or embodying, the blood of Christ.

CONSECRATION: The act by which a bishop makes something sacred.

CONVENT: A female monastery, housing nuns.

CROSS: Symbol of the Christian faith manifesting the promise of the redemption of humanity through Christ's death.

CRUCIFIXION: Death due to the nailing or binding of the hands and feet to a cross.

CRUSADES: A series of wars, taking place between the eleventh and fourteenth centuries, waged by European Christians to recover the Holy Land from Islam.

DEVIL'S ADVOCATE: The member of the Congregation of the Causes of Saints in the Vatican who critically investigates a candidate for sainthood.

DIOCLETIAN: Roman emperor 284—305, known for his spectacular persecutions of Christians toward the end of his reign.

DOCTORS OF THE CHURCH: Saints renowned for their theological brilliance and their influence on church doctrine. They number around thirty.

ECCLESIASTIC: Member of the clergy.

EPISCOPAL: Relating to a bishop or government by bishops.

EUCHARIST: The main act of worship in the Christian church, also called Mass.

FOURTEEN HOLY HELPERS: A group of fourteen saints invoked for their sensitivity and responsiveness to certain ailments and predicaments. Especially popular in the Middle Ages, their cult reached its zenith during the plague.

GRIDIRON: A grated metal frame used for roasting.

HABIT: Clothes worn by members of a religious order.

HERMIT: One who chooses to live alone to devote her- or himself to meditation, mortification, and prayer.

HUNDRED YEARS' WAR: 1337—1453. A momentous war between the English and French over territory in what is now France.

LITURGY: A service, or list of rites, prescribed for public worship.

MARTYR: Literally means "witness," but most commonly refers to someone who chooses death rather than denial of his or her faith.

MASS: The liturgy and celebration of the Eucharist.

MAXENTIUS: Son of Maximian; Roman emperor (306—312) following Diocletian. A persecutor of Christians.

MAXIMIAN: Ceasar (second only to the emperor) to Diocletian; father of Maxentius.

MITRE: The headdress of a bishop.

MONASTERY: The house sheltering a religious community; generally refers to a cloistered organization of males, or monks.

MONK: A male member of a religious community who has taken vows of chastity, poverty, and obedience.

MONSTRANCE: A vessel, usually made of gold or silver, that holds the Host (see Communion).

NUN: A female member of a religious community who takes simple or solemn vows and devotes herself to contemplation and perfection.

ORIGINAL SIN: The repercussions of the first sin, in which Adam and Eve disobeyed God and ate the fruit from the Tree of Knowledge. Many monks and nuns strive to achieve something of the purity known to Adam and Eve before Original Sin.

PASSION: The suffering of Christ on the Cross, but also encompasses his activities during the "Holy Week" between when he entered Jerusalem on Palm Sunday and his Crucifixion on Good Friday.

POOR CLARES: The Sisters of Saint Clare, or the Second Order of Saint Francis, founded in Assisi in 1212. An enclosed, contemplative, and severe community devoted to prayer, mortification, poverty, and meditation.

POPE: Heir and successor to Saint Peter, the pope has supreme authority over the Church as bequeathed to him by Christ.

PREMONSTRATENSIANS: A religious order also called the Norbertines after Saint Norbert, their founder.

RELICS: The bodily remains of dead saints or the instruments of their torture and death. They are often built into an altar of a church. Relics were often separated and dispersed, or translated, to other locations.

RULE: Regulations set down for the conduct of members of religious orders. Strictures can vary from abstinence of meat and strict enclosure to vows of poverty, manual labor, and chastity.

SACRAMENT: There are seven sacraments, or sacred obligations, that manifest divine grace. Baptism, Confirmation, Confession, Communion, and Extreme Unction are neccesary for all catholics. The sacraments of Holy Orders and Matrimony, being mutually exclusive, are optional.

SCRIP: A knapsack worn by a pilgrim.

SEAMLESS COAT: The seamless robe Christ wore when he was crucified. Made for him when he was a child, the robe supposedly grew with the man.

STAFF: A walking stick carried by pilgrims.

STATIONS OF THE CROSS: Episodes of Christ's journey to Calvary, often depicted in images or statuary inside a church or on the road to a church. At each station a worshiper might kneel and meditate about the event shown. There are fourteen authorized stations: 1) Sentencing by Pilate, 2) the Cross is given, 3) Jesus stumbles, 4) he meets his mother, Mary, 5) Simon is ordered to take the Cross, 6) Saint Veronica wipes his face, 7) he stumbles again, 8) he tells the women of Jerusalem not to weep, 9) he stumbles again, 10) he is disrobed, 11) he is nailed to the Cross, 12) he dies, 13) his body is taken from the Cross, 14) he is entombed.

STIGMATA: Bruises or open, bleeding wounds that appear on the feet, hands, side, and forehead of the recipient, like the five wounds of Jesus.

VALERIAN: Roman emperor, 253—260.

ART CREDITS

Page 155: *Saint Lucy* (detail), Francesco del Cossa. Samuel H. Kress Collection, © 1993 National Gallery of Art, Washington, after 1470

Page 133: *Saint Martin and the Beggar*, El Greco, Widener Collection, © 1993 National Gallery of Art, Washington, 1597/1599

Page 94: *Saint John in the Desert*, Domenico Veneziano, Samuel H. Kress Collection, © 1993 National Gallery of Art, Washington, c. 1445

Page 33: *Saint Apollonia*, Workshop of Piero della Francesca, Samuel H. Kress Collection, © 1993 National Gallery of Art, Washington, before 1470

Page 27: *Saint Anthony Leaving His Monastery* (detail), Sassetta, Samuel H. Kress Collection, © 1993 National gallery of Art, Washington, c. 1440

Page 66: *Saint Veronica*, Hans Memling, Samuel H. Kress Collection, © 1993 National Gallery of Art, Washington, c. 1470/1475

Page 49: *Saint George and the Dragon,* Sodoma, Samuel H. Kress Collection, © 1993 National Gallery of Art, Washington, probably 1518

Page 85: *The Death of Saint Clare*, Master of Heiligenkreuz, Samuel H. Kress Collection, © 1993 National Gallery of Art, Washington, c. 1410

With the exception of the aforementioned, the art that appears in this book has been culled from various public domain sources.

BIBLIOGRAPHY

Attwater, Donald. *The Penguin Dictionary of Saints.* London, England: Penguin Books, 1965.

Bentley, James. *A Calendar of Saints: The Lives of the Principal Saints of the Christian Year.* London, England: Orbis Book Publishing, 1986.

SAINT PHILLIP

Butler, Samuel. *Lives of the Saints, concise edition.* Michael Walsh. San Francisco: HarperSanFrancisco, 1991.

Coulson, John. *The Saints.* New York: Guild Press, 1958.

Farmer, David Hugh. *The Oxford Dictionary of Saints.* 2d ed. Oxford, England: Oxford University Press, 1987.

James, William. *The Varieties of Religious Experience.* New York: New American Library, 1958.

La Vie des Saints. Paris, France: P. Faivre Imprint.

McGinley, Phyllis. *Saint-Watching.* New York: Crossroads Publishing Company, 1969.

Ponsonailhe, Charles. *Les Saints par les Grands Maitres.* Tours, France: Alfred Mame et Fils.

Waddell, Helen. *The Desert Fathers.* Ann Arbor, Michigan: The University of Michigan Press, 1957.

Wescott, Glenway. *A Calender of Saints for Unbelievers.* New Haven, Connecticut: Leete's Island Books, 1932 and 1976.

Index

5. Pendant une maladie grave, St Jérôme lui apparaît et lui prodigue les consolations célestes. Il lui annonce pour l'avenir de grands travaux et de grandes souffrances à supporter pour l'amour de Jésus-Christ.

7. Ces songes mystérieux reçoivent enfin leur accomplissement. St François-Xavier, sur l'ordre de St Ignace, s'embarque pour les Indes suivi de deux jeunes religieux qu'il vient de donner à la Compagnie.

6. Dans un autre songe Xavier voit ses épaules chargées

8. Son arrivée dans les Indes est le signal de nombreux miracles. Un jour on lui amène un possédé. Il tire